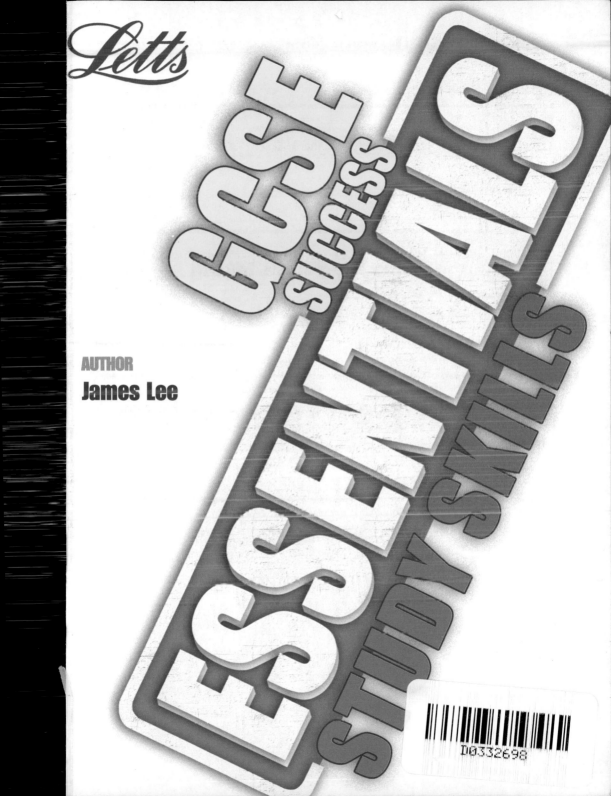

Letts

AUTHOR
James Lee

GCSE SUCCESS

ESSENTIALS

STUDY SKILLS

D0332698

Contents

Revising subjects

The exams

Contents

Developing better study skills

As you know, a good set of GCSE grades will provide you with a passport to further education. In addition, good grades give a strong sense of self-confidence in your capacity to study and to revise effectively, that will remain with you for the rest of your life. It is therefore really worth preparing as well as you can for your GCSEs – by starting your revision earlier rather than later, by staying positive throughout, and by developing better study skills.

As will become increasingly apparent as you work through this book, one of the beauties of study skills is that they take so many different forms. Some relate to managing yourself (e.g. time management and stress management), others are about the nuts and bolts of revision (e.g. reading and note-taking techniques), and there are other tools to use in specific situations (e.g. for particular subjects, for completing project work or for revising with a group of friends). Above all else, always bear in mind that study skills are meant to make studying more effective, more satisfying and more fun!

When developing better study skills, it is especially important to recognise that we all have unique learning styles. Some ways of learning and studying suit some people better than others. As you try out the various techniques and exercises outlined in this book, be sure to keep a mental note of which approaches help you most. Once you have finished this book, keep coming back to read through the various sections again. This will ensure that you strengthen your study skills in the run-up to your exams.

Good luck!

The structure of this book

This book is broadly divided into 5 topics. Together they introduce readers to a whole range of different principles and techniques.

- **Managing yourself and your time** begins with a section on goal-setting and getting started on your revision. This is followed by advice on how best to manage your time. The final part deals with how to reduce stress levels and manage your emotional state.
- **Memory, reading and note-taking** introduces a range of techniques to use when faced with the task of studying and revising GCSE topics. It begins with a section on ways to improve your memory, and then introduces some principles of effective reading, before clarifying how to use summary shapes and summary maps when taking revision notes.
- **Group work, project work and using ICT** gives a broader perspective on study skills. It begins with a section offering advice on how best to revise with friends and peers. It moves on to look at completing project work and, in particular, discusses how to conduct small-scale research projects. The final section discusses ways to use ICT when revising.
- **Revising subjects** gives some examples of how to apply the principles and techniques already introduced when revising specific subject areas. The subjects covered in this unit are: English, Maths, Science, Languages, History and Geography.
- **The exams** consists of a single but important final section that takes a leap forward to your GCSE exams and offers some hints on developing better exam techniques.

Now have a skim through the various sections of this book before taking a closer look at each chapter.

LET'S BEGIN

A wise man once said that the only important choice of the day is whether or not to get out of bed in the morning! Getting started on your revision is a bit like getting out of bed in the morning. You *could* put the alarm on snooze, delay it and delay it and delay it just a few more days – but you'll feel so much better about yourself if instead you get started early. This unit will help you to get started on your revision.

THE REFLECTIVE CYCLE

A cycle has a beginning, a middle, an end and repeats itself. For example, we could see each day as a cycle (morning, afternoon, evening, night), each week as a cycle (Monday, Tuesday, Wednesday…), and each year as a cycle (spring, summer…).

Rather than viewing the time between now and the end of your exams as one hard slog, it is helpful to break down your revision into a set of short cycles. Each of these cycles is known as a **reflective cycle** because it requires you to reflect on the progress that you have made:

- The beginning of the reflective cycle involves **vision** (e.g. to clarify the topics that you intend to revise today).
- The middle involves action (e.g. to muster up the discipline and concentration required to revise those topics).
- The end involves evaluation (e.g. to write in your journal or discuss with a friend the topics that you have revised).

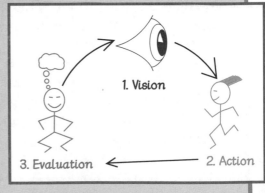

1. Vision

3. Evaluation

2. Action

1. VISION

Positive visualisation exercises are used by sportspeople to help them to focus on their goals. Have a go at applying them to your revision.

Early each morning and just before you go to sleep, find a quiet place, close your eyes, breathe deeply and count from ten to one. Now imagine yourself sitting down and feeling relaxed and concentrated. You are enjoying your revision in the place where you would normally revise. Take some more deep breaths and imagine yourself sitting in the room where you will take your exams. You are feeling relaxed, confident and all of the right questions are turning up. Take a couple more deep breaths and imagine yourself opening a letter confirming that you have been awarded fantastic GCSE grades!

2. ACTION

Some students are procrastinators. If on Monday they are given work to complete by Friday, then they start it on Thursday night or on the way to school on Friday morning! Complete tasks early and start to think about and write down what helps you to keep on schedule. For example:

- Start the day 30 minutes earlier and use this time to help you to catch up on homework that is pending or overdue.
- Give yourself treats for completing goals.
- Reorganise your room.
- Keep in close contact with a (disciplined) friend so that you can mentor and coach each other.

3. EVALUATION

Perhaps the most important part of the reflective cycle is the process of regularly evaluating how your revision is progressing. For example, you might ask a friend to test you on topics you have been revising, or you might keep a revision journal.

KEEPING A REVISION JOURNAL

Each evening, complete an entry in a revision journal. This will offer you the opportunity to review topics that you have been revising and will provide you with a sanctuary when, whatever else happened that day, you can let off steam by expressing how you are feeling.

SOME ADVICE ON GOOD JOURNAL-WRITING

1 Your journal can be any size. You might, for example, use an A5 notepad, an A4 notebook or an A3 sketchpad.
2 To respect this journal as your own creation, spend some time designing its cover around a theme relating to the successful completion of your exams (e.g. freedom).
3 Begin the first page or two with something that you find really motivating (e.g. a list of things that you are going to do in the summer after your exams have finished).
4 Follow the same format when completing each entry (e.g. date, how I'm feeling, topics that I revised today, what I found most difficult to revise, what I found most interesting, questions I need to ask, any other reflections).
5 You could illustrate your journal with doodles, jokes, poems and snippets from magazines.
6 Allocate a certain amount of time in which to complete each entry (e.g. 10–20 minutes).
7 Set aside time to review previous entries (e.g. Friday evening).
8 Once your exams have finished, symbolically recycle or burn your journal to mark the end of a significant phase of your life.

AN EXAMPLE OF A JOURNAL ENTRY

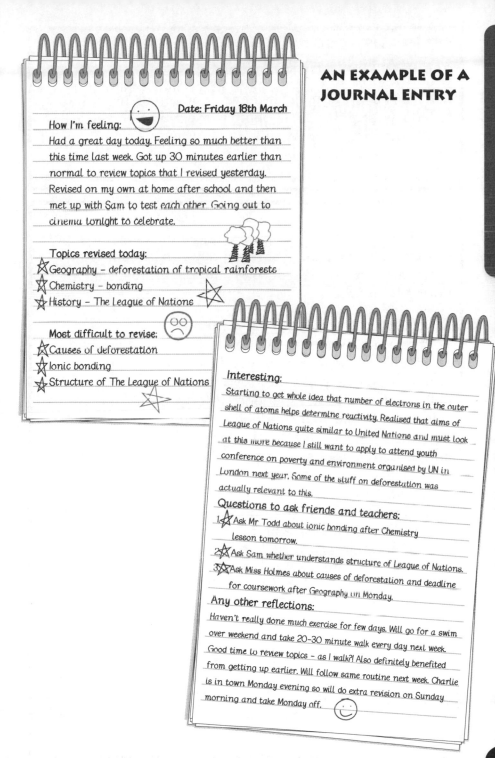

Date: Friday 18th March

How I'm feeling:

Had a great day today. Feeling so much better than this time last week. Got up 30 minutes earlier than normal to review topics that I revised yesterday. Revised on my own at home after school and then met up with Sam to test each other. Going out to cinema tonight to celebrate.

Topics revised today:

Geography – deforestation of tropical rainforests

Chemistry – bonding

History – The League of Nations

Most difficult to revise:

Causes of deforestation

Ionic bonding

Structure of The League of Nations

Interesting:

Starting to get whole idea that number of electrons in the outer shell of atoms helps determine reactivity. Realised that aims of League of Nations quite similar to United Nations and must look at this more because I still want to apply to attend youth conference on poverty and environment organised by UN in London next year. Some of the stuff on deforestation was actually relevant to this.

Questions to ask friends and teachers:

1. Ask Mr Todd about ionic bonding after Chemistry lesson tomorrow.

2. Ask Sam whether understands structure of League of Nations.

3. Ask Miss Holmes about causes of deforestation and deadline for coursework after Geography on Monday.

Any other reflections:

Haven't really done much exercise for few days. Will go for a swim over weekend and take 20-30 minute walk every day next week. Good time to review topics – as I walk?! Also definitely benefited from getting up earlier. Will follow same routine next week. Charlie is in town Monday evening so will do extra revision on Sunday morning and take Monday off.

SET REALISTIC GOALS

One way to manage your stress levels in the early phases of your revision is to focus on setting, achieving and reviewing short-term goals that can be completed within a few days. Once this initial phase is over you will feel confident enough to set additional targets. For now, though, focus on building your confidence by getting a few days of work under your belt.

THE FIRST SEVEN DAYS

Here is an example of a simple programme that you might want to follow for the first seven days. These suggested times may need to be reduced if this plan is followed during term time.

Day 1 (2–3 hours)

Confidence comes from experience. Even if every friend and family member reminds you how intelligent you are and how capable you are of revising, you simply won't believe this until you experience it for yourself. In order to refresh and build your confidence, begin your revision on a day when you have plenty of spare time (e.g. a weekend) and revise two topics that you find most interesting from your favourite subject. At the end of Day 1, ask somebody to test you on these topics, complete a revision journal entry and have a read through some of the later sections of this book to get some hints on core revision techniques such as note-taking.

Day 2 (3–4 hours)

Having proved to yourself that you are not so bad at studying and revising after all, set aside plenty of time to design your revision journal. You could also: begin work on the creation of a timetable; review topics that you revised yesterday; complete a revision journal entry; meet with a friend to discuss how best to approach your revision and, in particular, how you can best help each other to revise over the coming weeks and months.

Day 3 (2–3 hours)

Get up 30 minutes earlier than usual. Finish designing your journal and timetable and revise a topic from your least favourite subject. Complete a journal entry. Take care to record which areas you found difficult to understand when revising today. Make a note of someone you could speak to on a regular basis to get help with this subject (e.g. your teacher or a classmate).

Day 4 (2–3 hours)

Continue with your routine of getting up 30 minutes earlier. Start the day with a positive visualisation exercise. Revise two topics. Take a 20–30 minute walk and use this time to review topics you have been revising over recent days by talking through them as you walk. Complete your journal entry and another visualisation exercise just before you go to sleep.

Day 5 (2–3 hours)

Continue with your morning routine. Revise two more topics. Meet up with a friend to discuss topics you have revised over the last few days. Complete your revision journal entry and another visualisation exercise before you go to sleep.

Day 6 (1–2 hours)

Continue with your morning routine. Revise two more topics. Read through some further sections of this book and complete a journal entry to review this week and to decide whether to make changes to next week's routine. Take the evening off to celebrate!

Day 7 (30 minutes)

Have a bit of a lie-in but continue with your morning visualisation exercise soon after you wake up. Don't complete any formal revision today and try to get out of the house and do something refreshing. Towards the end of the day, use your journal to review your routine and goals for next week.

Time management

MAKING YOUR REVISION A PRIORITY

1   A long tree trunk has been laid out in a park and you are offered £1,000 if you manage to walk from one end to the other without falling off. Would you have a go?

2   The same tree trunk is balanced across the summit of a giant waterfall. Would you still have a go for £1,000?

3   Finally, this trunk is balanced across the same waterfall but someone is holding your friend hostage at the other side and threatens to throw him/her into the waterfall if you don't walk across. Would you try?

In terms of the next few months, place these activities in order from 1 (the most important) to 10 (the least important):

- Socialising with my friends
- Looking after my appearance
- Planning my next summer holiday
- Contributing towards local charitable projects
- Spending time with my parents
- Earning some extra cash
- Keeping fit/playing sports
- Finding/spending time with a/my partner
- Watching TV
- Revising for my exams.

The exercises above are about your values and your priorities. When we say that we don't have time to do something, often this is not strictly true. Instead, we don't see it as a priority. Do you currently view your revision as a high enough priority? Are you being too strict on yourself?

Good time managers are good at asserting their priorities. For example, if a friend asks you to go to the cinema then you will need to assert yourself with a response such as: 'Not today because I need to work. How about at the weekend?'

You should not, however, view your revision as your only priority. It is important that you also keep fit and fresh. At times you will therefore need to assert (e.g. to parents) that you need to rest, to play sport or to go out with friends.

BEGINNING TO ORGANISE YOUR TIME

Like being asked to recruit and train a football team, or write and direct a play, or organise an art exhibition, or market a new pop-band, revising for GCSEs is best viewed as a project that needs to be managed. An important project management skill is the ability to create good plans. When revising, this means creating good revision timetables.

SOME INITIAL QUESTIONS

The best timetables are **realistic** and **flexible**. When creating timetables, begin therefore by answering some important questions:

1. How many days are there until my first exam?
2. What is the maximum amount of time that I am willing to revise on a typical weekday, on a typical Saturday, and on a typical Sunday?
3. Are there any dates between now and my first exam when it will be very difficult or impossible for me to revise?
4. How many subjects am I studying?
5. How many topics am I expected to revise for each subject?

THE AMOUNT OF TIME AVAILABLE

Having answered these questions, you can now estimate the total number of hours available for revision between now and your first exam. You can calculate this (a diary and calculator are helpful here!) by following these steps:

1. Multiply the number of weekdays between now and your first exam by the time you intend to revise on weekdays.
2. Multiply the number of Saturdays between now and your first exam by the time you intend to revise on Saturdays.
3. Multiply the number of Sundays between now and your first exam by the time you intend to revise on Sundays.
4. Add these three totals together.
5. Subtract any time that is unavailable because it would be very difficult or impossible for you to revise on these days (e.g. you are playing in a sports tournament all day).

AMOUNT OF TIME FOR REVISION: AN EXAMPLE

Number of days until the first exam:

50 weekdays

10 Saturdays

10 Sundays

50
10
10

I will revise for:

70

2 hours on weekdays

3 hours on Saturdays

4 hours on Sundays

I cannot revise on:

5 weekdays

Calculations:

Weekdays: 50 (days) x 2 hours: 100 hours

Saturdays: 10 (days) x 3 hours: 30 hours

Sundays: 10 (days) x 4 hours: 40 hours

100
30
40

⭐Total: 170 hours

⭐170!

Unavailable: 5 (days) x 2 hours: 10 hours

⭐Total time available to revise: 160 hours

ALLOCATING TIME ACROSS SUBJECTS

Let's continue with our example.

Between now and your first exam you have 160 hours available for revision. You decide to assume, though, that you have underestimated the number of 'unavailable' Saturdays and Sundays, and therefore you round this figure down to 150 hours.

You are taking five subjects (English, Maths, French, Science and Geography) and, on average, you therefore have 30 hours available to revise each subject.

However, up until now you have spent most of your time preparing for English and Maths and you are less confident about your grasp of Science and Geography. You decide to divide up the 150 hours available as shown in the box below. There are 10 weeks until your first exam, so you also divide these figures by 10 to calculate the amount of time available for revising each subject each week.

Subject	Time (hours) to revise in total	Time (hours) to revise each week
English	20	2
Maths	20	2
French	30	3
Science	40	4
Geography	40	4
Total	150	15

ALLOCATING TIME ACROSS TOPICS

Before constructing a timetable, you now need to divide up this time between the various topics within each subject. Continuing with our example:

- You have allocated 40 hours to Geography.
- The Geography specification is made up of 15 topics.
- You have begun to revise five topics (tourism, trade and aid, geomorphic processes, settlement, energy resources).
- One topic you have not revised at all and is very long (weather and climate). You therefore decide to divide up the 40 hours of revision allocated to Geography as shown below.

1. Geomorphic processes	1 hour
2. River landscapes and hydrology	3 hours
3. Coastal landscapes	3 hours
4. Glacial landscapes	3 hours
5. Weather and climate	8 hours
6. Ecosystems	3 hours
7. Tectonic activity	3 hours
8. Population	3 hours
9. Settlement	1 hour
10. Urbanisation	3 hours
11. Energy resources	1 hour
12. Agriculture	3 hours
13. Industry	3 hours
14. Development, trade and aid	1 hour
15. Tourism	1 hour
Total	**40 hours**

NEXT...

A similar procedure can now be followed to divide up the time available to revise each of the other subjects that you are studying.

CONSTRUCTING WEEKLY TIMETABLES

You can now construct weekly timetables. You can follow one of two approaches here:

- You can create timetables on a week-by-week basis (e.g. each Sunday in advance of the week ahead).
- You can create all of the weekly timetables at the same time.

Returning to our scenario, here is an example of a weekly timetable. In addition to the topics noted, set aside 15–30 minutes every day to review topics that you have already revised.

Weekly timetable

	English (2 hours)	Maths (2 hours)	French (3 hours)	Science (4 hours)	Geography (4 hours)	TOTAL
Monday (2 hours)		Equations (1 hour)		Bonding (1 hour)		2 hours
Tuesday (2 hours)			Holidays (1 hour)		Tourism (1 hour)	2 hours
Wednesday (2 hours)	Newspapers (1 hour)			Waves (1 hour)		2 hours
Thursday (2 hours)			Grammar (1 hour)		Trade and aid (1 hour)	2 hours
Friday (2 hours)	Competing all day in the regional athletics championships 😊					0 hours
Saturday (3 hours)	Shakespeare (1 hour)	Vectors (1 hour)	Transport (1 hour)			3 hours
Sunday (4 hours)				Digestion (2 hours)	Weather (2 hours)	4 hours
TOTAL	2 hours	2 hours	3 hours	4 hours	4 hours	15 hours

REMEMBER

Timetables reduce stress levels by putting you in control of your revision. Stay calm if you get behind. By working towards the completion of all of your revision before your first exam, you will keep free all of the time between your exams, if necessary, to catch up on certain topics.

Stress management

CAUSES OF STRESS

Levels of stress experienced when revising and taking exams depend, to a certain extent, on **external circumstances**. Trying to revise in a hot and poorly ventilated room in which your little brother is watching TV at full volume and your sister is having an argument with her boyfriend is likely to prove very stressful. To this extent, taking positive action to create and maintain an environment that is conducive to effective revision (e.g. spacious, bright, cool and quiet) is a form of stress management.

Research suggests, however, that many students experience high levels of stress due to their **emotional response** to the task of preparing for and taking exams, rather than because of external factors alone. The ability to manage your emotional state is therefore a very important skill to develop when preparing for exams.

Two factors, in particular, appear to trigger stress:

- Major life changes (e.g. starting or ending a relationship, changing school, or moving house)
- A perceived lack of control over external circumstances (e.g. due to poor time management or low levels of confidence).

AVOIDING THE CAUSES OF STRESS

When preparing for exams:

 ● Try to avoid major life changes such as starting a new relationship.

 ● Apply the goal-setting and time management techniques outlined earlier in this book.

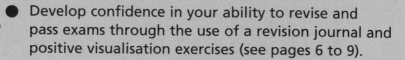 ● Develop confidence in your ability to revise and pass exams through the use of a revision journal and positive visualisation exercises (see pages 6 to 9).

EFFECTS OF STRESS

One way of thinking about stress is as a significantly heightened state of 'arousal'. A highly aroused physiological and emotional state (known as 'the fight or flight response') is helpful when facing imminent danger, but has a negative effect on performance in exams. The need to find an optimum state is well illustrated by the graph below. Very low levels of arousal are associated with low performance. As arousal levels increase so too do performance levels, until an optimum point after which performance reduces. A well-intentioned but highly anxious student can therefore perform as badly as a lazy and lethargic student. Make a note of activities that help you to restore an optimum emotional state of 'relaxed alertness'.

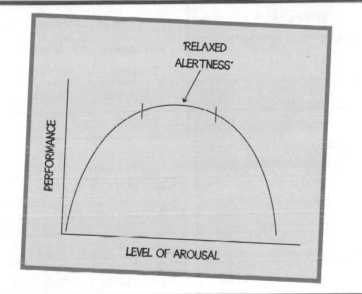

Inability to manage stress levels in the run-up to exams can have a wide range of consequences:

- **Emotional**, e.g. tension, anxiety and depression
- **Cognitive**, e.g. poor memory and difficulties concentrating
- **Physiological**, e.g. digestive and respiratory problems
- **Behavioural**, e.g. disrupted sleep patterns.

It is therefore really important to make your physical and mental health a high priority when preparing for exams.

EMOTIONAL INTELLIGENCE

One way to keep a close check on stress levels is to strengthen your **emotional intelligence** (EQ) – your capacity to manage and take responsibility for your own emotional state. Scientists now recognise that emotional intelligence is just as important a predictor of success in exams as other traditional measures of intelligence, such as IQ. If you have a high EQ then you can motivate yourself when you feel low or depressed and you can calm yourself down when you feel anxious or hyper. To help develop your EQ, periodically work through the five-stage exercise below. You can include exercises of this sort as entries in your revision journal (see opposite).

AN EXERCISE TO DEVELOP YOUR EMOTIONAL INTELLIGENCE

Pride → Humility
Jealousy → Generosity
Desire → Satisfaction
Greed → Discipline
Anger → Compassion

1. Recall an emotional situation
Identify recent circumstances when you had a strong experience of one of the 'red' emotions listed above.

2. Causes and triggers
Explain some of the causes and the triggers of this emotion.

3. Describe emotional state
Describe your experience of this emotion.

4. Consequences
Identify the consequences of your experience of this emotional state (both at the time and afterwards).

5. Know the antidote
Look at the 'blue' word alongside your chosen 'red' emotion. Describe how you might have experienced the situation differently if you had shown more of this emotion.

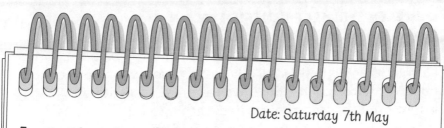

Date: Saturday 7th May

Emotional intelligence exercise

1. I got really angry last night.

2. As soon as I got back from school I went out to the cinema with friends. When I got in Dad had a real go at me. He accused me of being irresponsible and said that I'm not taking my exams seriously. This was so unfair as he doesn't realise that I've been working really hard all week.

3. When he was having a go at me I just froze. It felt as though I'd lost the ability to speak and I felt dizzy and confused.

4. I've been trying to revise all morning but I can't concentrate. I haven't been able to get rid of the anger I feel towards Dad and I can't concentrate on my revision. I feel useless and hate myself when I'm like this.

5. If I'd kept a better check on my emotions when Dad started going off on one then I would have recognised that what he was saying was making me angry. I would have tried harder to empathise with him and to recognise that he really loves me and wants me to do well in my exams but that he is frightened because he feels that he can't help. I would have explained that I've revised every evening this week. If he was still mad then I would have accepted that I am not responsible for his emotional state and I would have waited until he'd calmed down before having another chat with him.

DEVELOPING SELF-CONFIDENCE

One of the main causes of stress is an individual's sense that they are not able to control their circumstances. In the run-up to your exams, there are likely to be times when you feel that, however hard you try, life has presented you with an insurmountable set of obstacles. Perhaps you will set aside time to revise all weekend only to find that you come down with flu, or perhaps you will decide to get up early but forget to set your alarm and have to rush to catch the bus. The key is to ensure that you integrate obstacles and mistakes of this sort into the broader process of preparing for exams. In particular, regardless of any minor or major set-backs, you need to maintain a deeper confidence in your capacity to revise and to perform well in your exams.

SOME ADVICE ON MAINTAINING SELF-CONFIDENCE IN THE RUN-UP TO EXAMS

- Set yourself ambitious but realistic and achievable goals.
- When completing entries in your journal, make a list of all of your daily achievements, however small they might appear.
- Develop a sense of satisfaction and enjoyment in the whole process of preparing for exams (rather than focusing on results alone).
- Use positive visualisation exercises on a regular basis.
- Recognise mistakes as offering opportunities for feedback rather than as 'failures'.
- Recognise that your achievements are the result of your abilities and hard work rather than just a result of chance or good luck.
- Celebrate and reward yourself for short-term achievements.
- Complete tasks rather than leaving them unfinished.
- Revise and socialise with people who appreciate and value you.

DEVELOPING SUPPORT NETWORKS

Research suggests that students who benefit from positive support from a few close friends experience lower levels of stress than students who lack such support. Make sure that you avoid temptations and tendencies to isolate yourself in the run-up to exams. Similarly, take care to keep an eye on and support your friends and classmates. Identify other people who might be able to support you, such as family members, teachers and health professionals. There are plenty of informal and formal support systems (e.g. counselling services and youth workers) available to young people these days, so do feel absolutely free to make use of these.

Getting together with a friend specifically to discuss how you are progressing with revision

Going out for a drink or for a meal

Corresponding by phone, post or email

Communal activities to reduce stress

Going for short or long walks

Playing sports

LOOKING AFTER YOUR CLASSMATES

The personality types most at risk of experiencing high levels of stress are known as 'Type A' personalities and are characterised, in particular, by highly competitive, self-protective and aggressive attitudes towards other people when completing tasks. In contrast, students who adopt a more communal and caring attitude towards one another when preparing for exams tend to experience lower levels of stress. It is therefore very important to view classmates as companions rather than as competitors and to make an effort to maintain close friendships in advance of exams. This will ensure you are provided with the social support that you require while preparing for and completing your GCSEs.

Using mnemonics

A QUICK MEMORY TEST

A **mnemonic** is something that helps you to remember information. To help you understand the principles underpinning the use of mnemonics, give yourself 30 seconds to try to remember the following 15 words. Then try to write down as many as you can.

Warehouse

Brother

Mop

Tea

Mobile

Surfboard

Lipstick

Water

Mirror

Wall

Desert

Snake

Wind

Rainbow

Diamonds

TRY AGAIN

Did you remember all 15 words? Now read through the following story. Try to recount it to a friend or family member, or aloud to yourself (if no one else is around).

You wake up to find yourself in a huge **warehouse**. The voice of big **brother** suddenly asks you to pick up the **mop** at the other end of the factory and to clean the whole factory floor. You work all morning but then you become tired so you sit down on a bench to have a cup of **tea**. As you drink your tea your **mobile** phone rings. You look at the screen and there is an advert of a girl carrying a **surfboard**. Suddenly she breaks through the screen, sits down beside you, puts on some **lipstick**, throws a glass of **water** into your face, smashes a **mirror** and then jumps through the factory **wall**. You follow her and discover that you are in the middle of an enormous **desert**. There is nothing to see other than a **snake** that slithers towards you. As it gets closer the **wind** begins to blow very strongly. You put your hand down to stroke the snake and it transforms into a **rainbow** and a bag of **diamonds**.

Read through the list of words one more time before trying to recall them once again. This time have a go at remembering all 15 in the correct order.

PRINCIPLES TO FOLLOW WHEN USING MNEMONICS

Symbols

The manipulation of **symbols** allows us to represent information in simple and memorable ways. To remember, for example, that at the end of World War 1 a peace conference took place in Paris, you could think of a dove (a symbol of peace) flying over the Eiffel Tower (a symbol of Paris).

Outstanding

We are more likely to remember mnemonics that are **outstanding**. In the story there was therefore a 'huge' warehouse, an 'enormous' desert and shocking experiences such as a girl who threw water in your face, smashed a mirror and then jumped through a wall.

Links

Mnemonics make clear **links** between symbols. To remember, for example, the link between the depletion of the ozone layer and increased rates of skin cancer in Australia, you could think of a kangaroo (for Australia) that takes its jacket off (symbolising that it is no longer protected by the ozone layer) to reveal that it has blotchy white skin (for skin cancer).

All five senses

Mnemonics are easier to remember when they evoke **all five senses**. As you read the story you might, for example, have imagined the smell of freshly brewed tea, the taste of water thrown in your face, the sight of a snake transforming into a rainbow, the touch on your skin of a strong wind, and the sound of big brother's voice.

Repetition

We also remember mnemonics through **repetition**. Good ways of repeating and reviewing mnemonics are:

- Explaining them to friends.
- Keeping a written record of them using creative note-taking techniques based on the use of symbols and colour.
- Taking short 'memory walks' where you test your memory of various mnemonics as you walk.

AN EXAMPLE: MEMORISING HISTORICAL FACTS

What was agreed at the Yalta Peace Conference in February 1945?

- *Germany would be demilitarised.*
- *War criminals would be punished.*
- *Germany would be divided into four separate zones under the control of Britain, France, Russia and the USA.*
- *Russia would join the war against Japan.*
- *The United Nations would replace the League of Nations.*

1. Begin by choosing a symbol that represents this event and that you can use as the foundation for the rest of the mnemonic. In this case, the event was a peace conference in Yalta (a town on the coast of the Black Sea). You could therefore base your mnemonic around a black (to remind you of the Black Sea) dove (representing peace).

2. Use characteristics of this **base symbol** to help structure your mnemonic. Doves can fly. You could therefore structure this mnemonic around a black dove's journey between different places.

3. Choose symbols that remind you of facts: a broken gun (symbolising demilitarisation); a jailer's key (representing punishment); a cake (reminding you of the division of Germany into zones); a shredded Japanese flag that is saturated with vodka (symbolising Russia's declaration of war against Japan); and a blue peacekeepers' helmet (representing the creation of the United Nations).

4. Now create a series of evocative images that link together these symbols. Imagine, for example, that the dove picks up the trigger of the broken gun in its beak and drops this in the palm of a jailer's hand. In exchange, he gives her some keys which she carries to a woman who is just about to cut up her birthday cake. In return the woman gives the dove a shredded flag. The dove flies back home and uses this flag to help build her nest in a discarded blue helmet.

AN EXAMPLE: MEMORISING GEOGRAPHICAL CONCEPTS

UN concepts of sustainable development

- **Interdependence:** *actions influence other people locally and globally.*
- **Citizenship:** *rights and responsibilities.*
- **Future:** *responsibilities include the protection of future generations.*
- **Diversity:** *respect for cultural, social, economic and biological diversity.*
- **Equity:** *respect for quality of life, equity and justice for all.*
- **Sustainability:** *monitoring development and change.*
- **Uncertainty:** *we cannot predict with certainty the outcome of our actions.*

1. These concepts relate to the topic of sustainable development. You could therefore base and structure your mnemonic around a symbol that represents the management of growth, such as a gardener.
2. Professional gardeners sometimes work in very large and elaborate gardens. You could therefore situate and structure this mnemonic in and around a beautiful large garden.
3. In order to remember and catch the essence of these concepts you could use the following symbols: a domino (to symbolise interdependence, as in the domino effect); a passport (to symbolise citizenship); a crystal ball (to symbolise concern for the future); a multicoloured flower (to represent diversity); a clenched fist (to symbolise equity and justice); a pair of spectacles (to symbolise monitoring change); and a question mark (to represent uncertainty).
4. In order to create a connected and evocative mnemonic from these symbols you could imagine that the gardener is digging in the vegetable patch when he discovers a golden domino. He excitedly places the domino in his passport and throws both onto the bonfire. A crystal ball suddenly rolls out of the bonfire and the gardener picks this up and stares into it. All that he can see is a multicoloured flower. The gardener clenches his fist with joy, puts on his spectacles and draws a giant red question mark on the crystal ball before throwing it back into the fire.

AN EXAMPLE: MEMORISING FOREIGN VOCABULARY

Days of the week in German

Montag *Dienstag* Mittwoch *Donnerstag*

Freitag **Samstag** **Sonntag**

1. All of the days, other than Mittwoch (Wednesday), end with the syllable 'tag'. You could therefore structure your mnemonic around the symbol of a shopping tag.
2. Imagine seven giant tags hanging off a long pole in your bedroom. On Monday you pull the first tag and nothing happens. **Montag** has the same first syllable as Monday.
3. When you pull the second tag on Tuesday a celebrity with the name Dean, or someone that you know with this name, walks into the room and signs the tag to proclaim it as his own (**Dienstag**).
4. On Wednesday there is no tag because Mittwoch does not end in 'tag'. Instead there is a piece of string with a brightly coloured mitten (Mitt) at one end and a brand new wok (woch) at the other.
5. On Thursday Madonna walks into the room and signs the next tag to claim it as her own (**Donnerstag**).
6. Madonna hangs around in your room until Friday when she pulls the next tag and uses the wok to fry her bra (**Freitag**).
7. On Saturday morning you are having a lie-in when Fat Sam the gangster bursts in shooting tomatoes everywhere. He then signs his name in tomato juice on the tag to proclaim it as his own (**Samstag**) before leaving via the window.
8. On Sunday peace returns. You wake up, pull the seventh tag and look out of your window. On a far-away hill stands a boy smiling as the sun shines down. The boy is your son. Sunday is **Sonntag**.

AN EXAMPLE: MEMORISING CHEMICAL PROCESSES

Reactivity

The reactivity series
Some metals are more reactive than others:

Not reactive at all –	**gold**
Not very reactive –	**tin**
Quite reactive –	**aluminium**
Very reactive –	**potassium**

Some reactions

When metals react with oxygen a metal oxide is formed.

When metals react with water a metal oxide (or hydroxide) and H_2 are formed.

When metals react with dilute acid a salt and H_2 are formed.

A mnemonic on the reactivity series could be based around the symbol of a big fire into which different objects are thrown with different effects.

1. When you throw a gold watch (**gold**) into the fire there is no effect because gold is not reactive at all.

2. When you throw a tin can (**tin**) into the fire there is a very slight crackling because tin is not very reactive.

3. When you throw an aluminium can (**aluminium**) into the fire there is a bang because aluminium is quite reactive.

4. When you throw a pot (**potassium**) into the fire there is a huge explosion because potassium is very reactive.

The three reactions mentioned are with oxygen, water and dilute acid. A mnemonic to help remember each reaction could be based on the symbols of an aluminium can (for metals) and three buckets (for the three types of reaction).

1. When an aluminium can is placed in an empty bucket (reaction with oxygen) it changes colour (forms an oxide).

2. When an aluminium can is placed in a bucket of water (reaction with water) it changes colour (forms an oxide or hydroxide) and lots of little 'H's float into space (releases hydrogen).

3. When an aluminium can is placed in a bucket of thick smelly liquid (reaction with dilute acid) it turns into table salt (forms a salt) and lots of little 'H's float into space (releases hydrogen).

Effective reading

USING A READING GUIDE

- Sit close to a friend or family member and look at one another face to face.
- Ask your partner to draw an imaginary circle with his/her eyes.
- Watch your partner's eye movements as he/she draws this circle.
- Ask your partner to follow the tip of your finger as you draw an imaginary circle in the air.
- Watch your partner's eye movements as they follow your finger.
- Swap around so that your partner watches your eye movements.

Did your partner's eyes draw a smoother circle with or without the guide? You should have found that when following a guide (in this case a finger) the eye movements were far smoother. Without a guide the eyes tend to wander around. The same is true of reading.

Always use a reading guide to direct the movement of your eyes. You can use any pointed object as a guide, but usually the most practical is a pencil or a fine-point pen. Don't use a bookmark because we tend to subconsciously read a few lines ahead and bookmarks block out our peripheral vision.

When using a guide you will typically direct your eyes to read from left to right. There are, however, different options depending on the purpose of your reading and the type of text that you are reading.

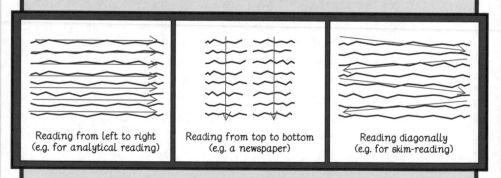

Reading from left to right
(e.g. for analytical reading)

Reading from top to bottom
(e.g. a newspaper)

Reading diagonally
(e.g. for skim-reading)

A NOTE ON READING LESS WELL-STRUCTURED TEXTS

Some texts are well-structured whereas others are less well-structured. The passage of text below is an example of a less well-structured text.

Multinational companies:

A controversial issue
Even though multinationals typically employ large numbers of people, relocation of operations to less economically developed countries (LEDCs), on the basis that the workers in these countries demand lower wages, is seen as exploitative.

Multinationals in the UK
Most UK-based multinationals are public limited companies. Multinationals typically employ large numbers of people, provide new technology and specialist expertise, and encourage innovative business practices.

Characteristics of multinationals
Multinational companies export profits and, despite their encouragement of innovative business practices, their imposition of working practices can lead to disputes with employees. They also expect employees in LEDCs to work for low wages. Multinationals use relocation of business operations to diversify.

It is important that you adapt your reading approach according to the style and structure of the text that you are reading. Less well-structured texts require a distinct approach because:

1. **The headings may not accurately reflect the text content.** For example, the second and third sections above mainly discuss the advantages and disadvantages of relocating business operations to other countries – but this is not obvious from the headings. Always assume that you can create better headings than those used in the text itself.

2. **Information is repeated.** In the example, information about low wages, innovative practices and employment of large numbers of people is repeated. Always read the whole passage in full first to avoid repeating yourself when taking notes.

3. **Some sentences are irrelevant.** For example, in paragraph 2 above, the fact that UK multinationals are public limited companies is not relevant to the main focus of the text (i.e. advantages of multinationals), and in paragraph 3 provision of opportunities to diversify is not relevant to the main focus (i.e. the disadvantages of multinationals). Focus only on relevant information.

DIFFERENT READING APPROACHES: SKIM-READING

If you are reading to develop an overview of a topic, or only to extract information related to a specific issue or topic, then **skim-reading** is the best technique. Here are some important principles for effective skim-reading.

1. Strict time constraints

Skim-reading is best suited to circumstances where you are required to read large amounts of text in short amounts of time (e.g. when reviewing topics you have already revised or when reading around before writing up coursework reports). When skim-reading, stick to strict time constraints. Whereas, for example, you might initially have spent 2 hours analysing a topic, set aside just 20 minutes to skim-read it at a later date.

2. Headings, sub-headings and graphs

Focus at first on reading the headings and sub-headings and on studying any diagrams, tables or graphs (especially the captions). It is also helpful to view the text as a jigsaw puzzle that needs to be completed. Much like starting a jigsaw puzzle by identifying the corner pieces and edges, start reading by identifying and linking together pieces of information that are of immediate and obvious relevance.

3. First and last paragraphs

The first few paragraphs often overview the content of a passage of text while the last few paragraphs typically summarise it. Having examined headings, diagrams, tables and graphs, read more carefully the first and last few paragraphs. Keep a piece of paper by your side to take rough notes as you read.

4. Key words and symbols

Read through the whole text from start to finish, brushing over anything that you still do not understand and taking occasional notes in the margins or on paper using only key words and symbols (see page 37). Work at pace to ensure that you do not become distracted. People typically sub-vocalise (speak aloud in their heads) as they read. When skim-reading, try to sub-vocalise more quietly and quickly than normal (like someone whispering instructions to you at lightning speed).

5. The summary

Look through your notes and give yourself, in no more than a couple of paragraphs, a couple of minutes to summarise the whole passage of text. Make an additional note of any information of particular interest and of concepts, issues or sections that you struggled to understand. If possible, take this opportunity to talk through your summary with someone else.

TRUST YOUR INTELLIGENCE

Read the following couple of sentences as slowly as you can, taking care to sound out each word as you read:

> Many investors in the stock market had raised money 'on the margin' (90% of cost of shares that they bought had been borrowed from banks). Recognition of economic decline led to 'panic-selling' and the Wall Street Crash of October 1929.

Now read the same passage more quickly. You should find that it was far easier to understand this passage when you read it more quickly. Trying to read 'slowly and carefully' can be a mistake, whereas reading more quickly can improve your comprehension. Some students don't realise that their mind is bored by the slow speed at which they read.

DIFFERENT READING APPROACHES: ANALYTICAL READING

If you are reading because you need to develop detailed memory and understanding of text, then **analytical reading** is the best technique. In these circumstances use the following seven-stage model to help guide and structure your reading.

1. Read through the whole passage

Read through the passage from start to finish to build up a big picture of the topic that you are studying. Pay particular attention to the title and to any sub-titles, diagrams, tables and graphs. When you have finished, reflect on what you have read and jot down any questions that emerge at this stage.

2. Use colour, key words and symbols

Colour

Highlight information by using different colours. You could, for example, use a different colour for each section or you could develop a coding system that uses red for very important information, blue for important information and green for quite important information.

Key words

As you read through the passage a second time, you should underline key words. Take care not to underline too many words though or you will end up underlining virtually the whole passage. Normally there is no need to underline more than three words per sentence. Bear in mind that in some sentences there are no key words at all.

Symbols

A symbol represents or reminds us of something else. For example, Big Ben might remind us of democracy or a pair of masks might remind us of the theatre. As you read through the passage of text, draw symbols in the margins to represent key information in each paragraph. You should end up with between one and six symbols per paragraph.

3. Make a summary sheet
The secret to effective note-taking is not to copy out everything in your own handwriting, but to use the colours, key words and symbols that you drew in the margins of the original passage to create a summary sheet such as a summary shape or a summary map (see pages 36–37).

4. Complete the summary sheet from memory
Once you have finished your summary sheet, talk through it by yourself or, ideally, with someone else. Look back at the original to correct any mistakes. Then, trace the outline (i.e. no words or symbols but the overall shape of the summary shape or branches of the summary map) before filling in this 'skeleton' from memory. Look back at the original and correct any mistakes for a final time.

5. Write up the passage from memory (optional)
Try to write up the passage that you have been learning from memory and in your own words or to teach it to someone else. Writing information in your own words, and teaching, improve memory and understanding.

6. Take a break
In order to allow your mind to assimilate information, it is important that you take regular breaks. You should take a 5–15 minute break every 60 minutes. Use these opportunities to get away from your desk, to have a cup of tea, to phone a friend or to go for a short walk.

7. Review, review, review
Some specialists suggest that if you don't review topics then you may forget as much as 80% within 24 hours and 98% within 7 days! Set aside 10–15 minutes every day to review topics that you have already revised. Early in the morning and just before you go to sleep are particularly good times for review.

Note-taking: Summary shapes

DEVELOPING A PORTFOLIO OF SUMMARY SHEETS

In the run-up to your exams you will spend a long time taking revision notes from textbooks, from handouts or from your own class notes. Instead of copying these out in your own words (you can copy out a whole book and still not remember or understand what you have written), try to work towards developing a portfolio of summary sheets.

For each topic, create summary sheets on plain A4, A3 or A2 paper. Instead of sentences, these sheets should use key words, symbols and colour to summarise and highlight important facts and concepts. This chapter introduces you to the use of summary shapes to help revise less complex texts. The next chapter then outlines the use of summary maps to help revise more complex texts.

USING ANNOTATIONS

Whatever text you are studying, it is very helpful to have the freedom to write annotations (e.g. key words or symbols) in the margins. Annotations are best written using a selection of colours, but if the texts that you are reading belong to a library then you may need to photocopy sections or to use a very light (e.g. 2H) pencil and then carefully erase all of your annotations before returning texts you have borrowed. Page 38 illustrates how you might use key words, symbols and colour to annotate text – in this case about the life of David Beckham.

KEY WORDS

You do not need to use sentences when writing revision notes. You do not, for example, need to write 'David Beckham married Posh Spice in Ireland' in order to remember this section of his life. Underlining the key words 'married' and 'Ireland' would be enough to trigger your memory. Similarly, you do not need to write 'Beckham's first child was called Brooklyn and was born in 1999'. Underlining the key word 'Brooklyn' and the date '1999' would be enough.

SYMBOLS

Symbols represent or remind us of something else. A symbol of Big Ben with the number '75' next to it will, for example, remind us that Beckham was born in London in 1975. Similarly, drawing a cap and a trophy with the number '02' above it will remind us that Beckham captained the England team during the 2002 World Cup.

COLOUR

When studying and revising, use a selection of fine-point coloured pens to discriminate and highlight information. Look again at the text on the life of Beckham. You can see that all of the key words or symbols referring to his personal life or family are underlined, written or drawn in blue. All of the key words and symbols referring to Beckham's career are underlined, written or drawn in red.

The Life of David Beckham

1. Born in North <u>London</u> on 2nd May <u>1975</u>.
2. First played for the <u>Manchester United</u> senior team at <u>17</u>.
3. Blamed for England's defeat in the <u>1998</u> <u>World Cup</u> after being sent off for a <u>foul</u> against an Argentinean player.
4. First child, <u>Brooklyn</u>, was born in March <u>1999</u>.
5. <u>Married</u> Posh Spice (Victoria Adams) in <u>Ireland</u> in July <u>1999</u>.
6. <u>Captained</u> the England team during the <u>2002</u> World Cup.
7. Second child, <u>Romeo</u>, was born in September <u>2002</u>.
8. Transferred to <u>Real Madrid</u> in summer of <u>2003</u>.

Which shape you use for your summary will depend on the number of sections into which you split the text. If, for example, you split a text into three sections then use a triangle; if you split it into four sections then use a square; if you split it into five or six sections then use a five-point or a six-point star; and if you split it into eight sections then use a circle. In the case of the life of Beckham, this has been split into eight sections and therefore we can use an eight-part **summary circle**.

A SUMMARY CIRCLE ON THE LIFE OF DAVID BECKHAM

Draw your summary shape on a plain piece of paper and fill it in with the key words, symbols and colours that you used to annotate the text itself. In the case of the life of Beckham, this will involve the use of an eight-part summary circle. The example below illustrates what this might look like once it has been completed.

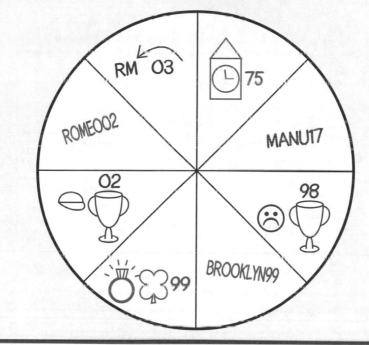

TEST YOURSELF

Once you have completed the shape, test yourself. For our Beckham example you could:

- Talk through Beckham's life aloud.
- Close your eyes and try to visualise the contents of the circle in your mind's eye.
- Try to fill in a blank eight-part circle that you have sketched on a rough piece of paper.
- Ask a friend or a member of your family to test you on Beckham's life.

You may well be surprised just how much you can remember!

THE LIFE HISTORY OF ANOTHER FAMOUS BECKS!
Having worked through a more topical example, have a go at transferring the study skills that you have learnt to the life history of another famous Becks. In this case, though, he was chancellor, archbishop of Canterbury and lived over 800 years ago!

The Life of Thomas Becket

H2 B £ 1. When <u>Henry II</u> became <u>king</u> in 1154 he chose Becket as <u>chancellor</u>.

2. At this time there were two law <u>courts</u> – <u>church</u> courts for members of the clergy and <u>royal</u> courts for everyone else.

3. In 1162 Henry II appointed Becket as <u>Archbishop</u> of Canterbury because he wanted him to help abolish the church courts.

4. Soon after being appointed archbishop Becket devoted himself to God and <u>refused</u> to abolish the church courts.

5. Henry II was furious and Becket <u>fled</u> abroad to live in <u>France</u>.

6. Becket <u>returned</u> from exile in France in 1170 but <u>angered</u> Henry II when he threatened to sack the Archbishop of York.

7. Four knights <u>murdered</u> Becket in Canterbury in December 1170.

8. <u>Pilgrims</u> visited Becket's <u>tomb</u> until it was destroyed in 1539.

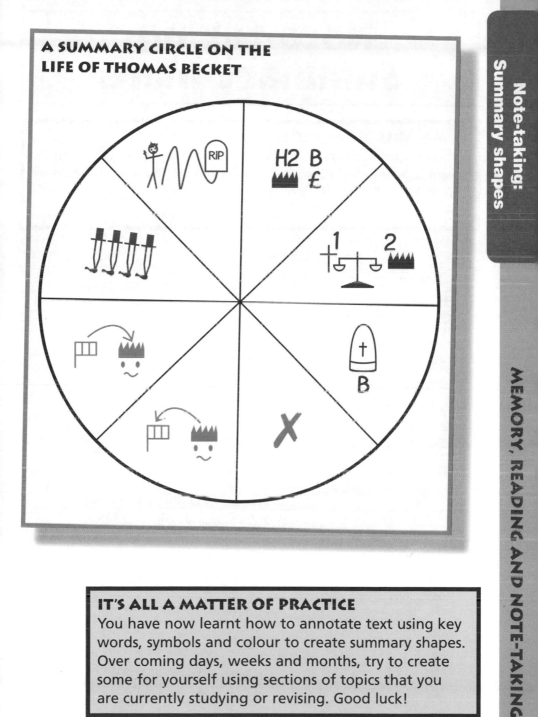

A SUMMARY CIRCLE ON THE LIFE OF THOMAS BECKET

IT'S ALL A MATTER OF PRACTICE

You have now learnt how to annotate text using key words, symbols and colour to create summary shapes. Over coming days, weeks and months, try to create some for yourself using sections of topics that you are currently studying or revising. Good luck!

Note-taking: Summary maps

SUMMARISING MORE COMPLEX TEXTS

When required to revise more complex texts, another option is to create summary maps. Like the creation of summary shapes (see pages 36–41), begin by annotating with key words, symbols and colour in the margins of the text as shown below.

1879!

Albert Einstein

EARLY

Early years

Einstein was born in Germany in 1879. He studied Maths and Physics at Zurich University. Einstein later worked as a Maths teacher and married a Serbian. They had two sons.

Zurich
Maths

PAPERS

Scientific impact:

At the age of twenty-six, Einstein published 3 important papers:

1. The first was about light. It highlighted that the photons that make up light have the properties of both particles and waves.

2. The second was about particles' movement in liquids. It showed that we can predict how particles move when they are placed in a liquid.

3. The third was about relativity. This established that the energy (e) of matter is determined by its mass (m) multiplied by the square of the velocity of light (c). This led to the famous equation $e = mc^2$.

$e = mc^2$

FAME

Fame

Einstein was famous amongst academics. He was made a professor in Prague and then Zurich. He was later elected to an academy in Berlin. Einstein also became an internationally famous symbol of intellect, progress and hope.

Prague
Berlin
Symbol

LATER

Later years

Einstein was Jewish and left Nazi Germany for Princeton University in USA. During World War 2 he encouraged Roosevelt to press ahead with atomic research. In later years he campaigned for disarmament. He died on 18th April 1955.

Atomic?!

18/4/55

RIP

CREATING SUMMARY MAPS

1. A central title

- Begin with a blank page of plain (not lined) A4, A3 or A2 paper.
- Turn the page so that it is in landscape layout and then write a title in the centre of the page (e.g. the word 'Einstein' or a picture to symbolise Einstein, such as a face with a crazy hairstyle!).
- Placing the title in the centre of the page emphasises that it is central to the topic.
- Enclose the title by drawing a shape around it (e.g. a circle, a square or a cloud).

2. Dividing up text into sections

- Divide up the text into 2–6 sections.
- The life of Einstein has already been divided into four sections (early years, scientific impact, fame, and later years). When studying and revising less-structured texts you will need to identify sections for yourself.
- Before taking any further notes, generate a rough impression in your mind's eye of the layout of your summary map (e.g. each of the four sections on Einstein is likely to take up roughly a quarter of the page).

3. Branching out

- Summary maps represent information like a tree branching out from the centre to the edges of the page.
- Begin at 'two o'clock' by drawing a thick branch and writing a single key word on top of this as a sort of sub-heading.
- To make best use of space on the page, draw curved (rather than straight) branches off this main branch and write on top of these using key words and symbols from the margins of the text.
- Repeat with all sections using colour throughout (see page 45).

4. Memorising summary maps

Summary maps provide concise and powerful summaries of complex topics. They are very helpful when reviewing topics you have already revised. An excellent form of review is to try to recall a summary map from memory:

- Look carefully at the original map for anything unique that might help you to remember its layout and content (e.g. the colours used).
- Pay attention to the title and to words on top of the main branches.
- Study carefully any groups of symbols (e.g. the wave made of dots, the beaker with the particle in the middle, the equation $e=mc^2$).
- Check for examples of repetition (e.g. the word 'Zurich' in the 'early' and 'fame' sections of the Einstein summary map).
- Close your eyes and try to see the summary map in your mind's eye.
- Try to describe the summary map to someone else.

5. Test yourself

- Place a blank piece of paper on top of the summary map and trace only the branches (i.e. no key words or symbols).
- Look through the original a final time and then complete the skeleton summary map from memory.
- In order to save time, use the same pen throughout and don't worry about neat handwriting (see page 46).
- Once you have completed as much as you can remember, look back at the original and use a different colour to correct any omissions or mistakes.

A SUMMARY MAP ON ALBERT EINSTEIN

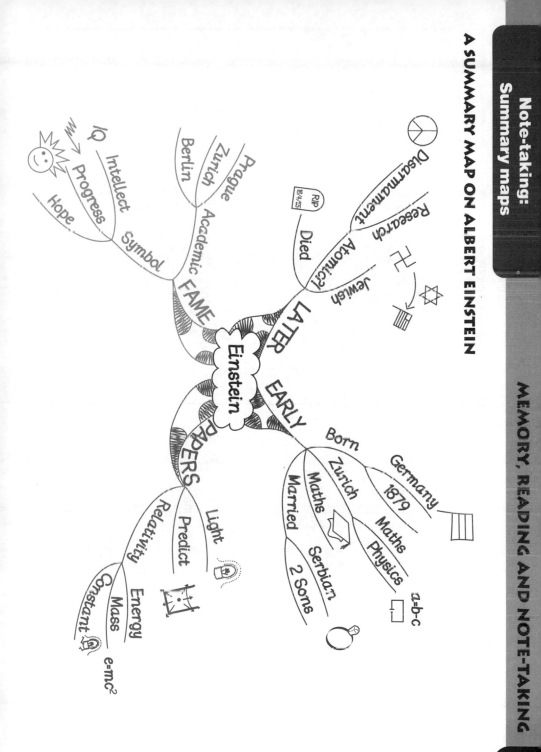

RECALLING THE SUMMARY MAP ON EINSTEIN FROM MEMORY

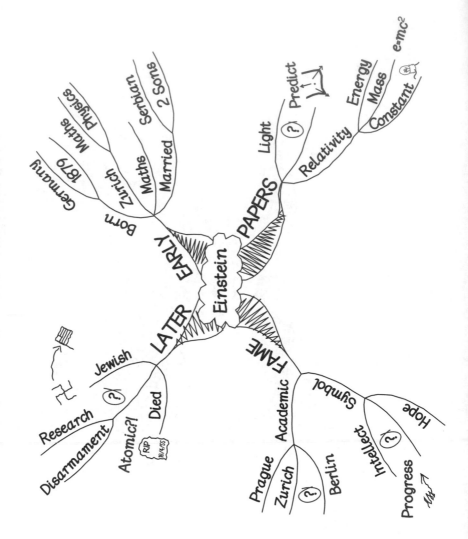

SUMMARISING LARGER TOPIC AREAS

Some topics are too large, at first, to be summarised on a single summary map and might therefore require, say, two to six summary maps instead. It is relatively easy, however, to group summary maps through translating central headings into main branches and main branches into subsidiary branches, etc. The example below illustrates how four summary maps could be condensed down to a single summary.

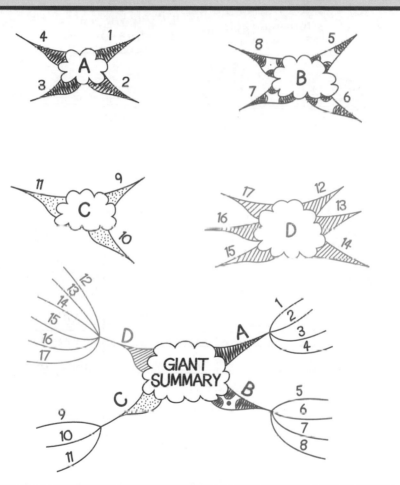

REMEMBER

Don't feel limited to using A4 paper alone. With large topic areas why not create giant summary maps on A3, A2 or A1 paper and stick these on your bedroom walls!

Revising with others

A LEARNING ANALOGY
The deeper that we process information (the more that we do with it) the more likely we are to remember and understand it.

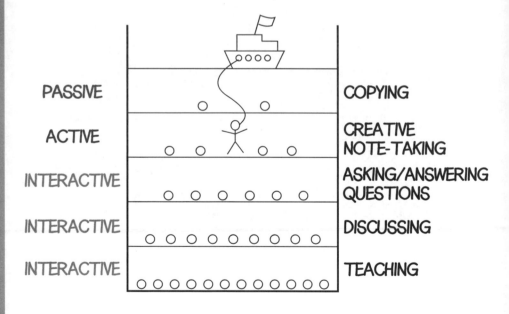

PASSIVE	COPYING
ACTIVE	CREATIVE NOTE-TAKING
INTERACTIVE	ASKING/ANSWERING QUESTIONS
INTERACTIVE	DISCUSSING
INTERACTIVE	TEACHING

INTERACTIVE LEARNING

The diagram opposite highlights that the most effective ways of learning involve working and interacting with others. The diagram is of a deep-sea pearl diver. The deeper that this diver goes the more pearls (of wisdom!) that he/she can find. This analogy represents the fact that the deeper that we 'process' information the more likely we are to remember and understand it. Let's examine this very important concept a bit further.

When presented with a passage of text to revise, we could type it out on our computer or copy it out in our own hand-writing. This is called passive learning. It is very inefficient, so there are few pearls (it is totally possible to copy out a whole book and still know nothing about it).

Active learning includes the use of more creative note-taking techniques (such as summary shapes and summary maps) that require us to think while taking notes. Active ways of learning are more effective and therefore there are more pearls at this level.

The most effective ways of learning (shown in the diagram as having the most pearls) are interactive (e.g. questioning, discussing and teaching).

CHECKLIST FOR INTERACTIVE REVISION

In the run-up to exams it is therefore absolutely essential that you take every opportunity to:

- Use creative note-taking techniques such as summary sheets.
- Ask and answer questions inside and outside of class.
- Participate in discussions inside and outside of class.
- Teach the topics that you are revising (e.g. to a member of your family or by pairing up with a friend).
- Stay 'on task' (e.g. when revising with friends, discuss topics you are revising rather than the party that you went to last night).

INTERACTIVE LEARNING IN CLASS

Teachers are normally pretty good at offering students opportunities to learn interactively in class (e.g. to participate in discussions). Classroom talk still tends, though, to be dominated by a few people. You will get much more out of classes if you actively participate in classroom talk.

CHECKLIST FOR INTERACTIVE CLASSES

Some advice on making the most of classes in the run-up to your exams:

- If you know that a particular topic is going to be covered during a particular class, then revise this the night before and arrive with a list of related questions to ask classmates or your teacher.
- Ask teachers to re-explain things that you don't understand.
- Always try to answer questions that the teacher asks, even if you are not sure whether or not you know the answer (just talking and thinking about the question and answer will help you to learn).
- If you are just too shy to ask questions during class, then get into the habit of asking teachers questions at the end of class.
- Encourage your classmates to stay on task when you are split into groups to work on collaborative exercises.
- Avoid sitting next to consistently disruptive students.
- Speak to your teachers in private if certain classmates intimidate or bully you for asking or answering questions.
- Respect your classmates for participating in class discussions and for asking and answering questions.
- Thank other students for their contribution to class discussions.

DEVELOPING BETTER WORKING RELATIONSHIPS

A key theme that emerges is the fact that your greatest resource in the run-up to exams is your relationship with other people. When developing better working relationships with classmates, teachers and parents, bear in mind four factors, known as the **wheel of needs**, that underpin a high rapport relationship.

If one section is missing then the wheel won't turn and the relationship won't work

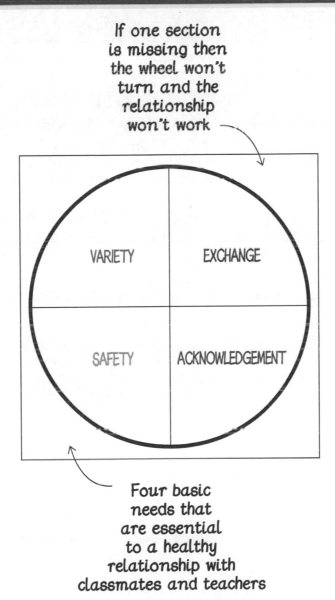

VARIETY

EXCHANGE

SAFETY

ACKNOWLEDGEMENT

Four basic needs that are essential to a healthy relationship with classmates and teachers

THE WHEEL OF NEEDS

Exchange

The first basic need is the provision of opportunities for **exchange**. Some people are very good listeners (receivers) and some people are very good talkers (givers). In high rapport relationships, both individuals are provided with opportunities to give and to receive. If you want to develop a better relationship with someone in your class (e.g. the smartest student!) then ask them for help or offer help. Asking people for help is a very good way of building friendships because it treats other people as valuable.

Acknowledgement

There are lots of ways to **acknowledge** other people. For example, we can thank them, compliment them, praise them or applaud them. Sometimes students are disruptive in class because they feel unacknowledged and may therefore calm down a bit if you acknowledge them more. If you want to develop a better relationship with a particular teacher then make an effort to thank them or to ask them some questions at the end of class.

Safety

Our basic need to feel **safe** means that it is really essential that you do not make classmates or teachers feel threatened by your presence (e.g. your language or body language). The best rule to follow here is public praise and private criticism. We should try to praise people in public places (e.g. in class) and only to criticise in private (e.g. to sort out any problems with individual classmates or teachers at the end of class in an environment where they will not feel humiliated by public criticism).

Variety

Sometimes relationships break down out of boredom! Individuals who bring appropriate humour, spontaneity and **variety** to interactions are often good at building high rapport relationships. Don't get too heavy or serious in the run-up to exams. Stay light and open.

REVISING WITH FRIENDS OUTSIDE OF CLASS

It is tempting to think that outside of class the top students do nothing but sit by themselves silently studying for hours on end in their bedroom or at their local library. Of course, when revising, you will need to develop the patience and concentration required to work alone for relatively long periods of time (no more than an hour without a break though). You must ensure, however, that revision sessions of this sort are complemented by regular revision with (well-motivated and disciplined) friends.

CHECKLIST FOR REVISING WITH FRIENDS

- A few days in advance of meetings, organise to revise the same topics so that you can discuss these together.
- Test each other on your memory of summary sheets that you have created over the last few days.
- Jointly create mnemonics to help memorise concepts/facts.
- Keep in close contact by phone and email to offer one another on-going help and support.
- Split up a topic into short sections. Study a section alone for a few minutes, discuss your memory and understanding of this section for a few minutes and then study another section by yourself for a few minutes, etc.
- Make a list of questions to ask one another at meetings.
- To create variety, try revising in different environments (e.g. at home, in a café or going for a walk).
- Find time to celebrate on-going achievements together!

Completing project work

YOUR COURSEWORK

A significant number of GCSE specifications now require students to complete coursework in the form of short research projects. You may, for example, be required to examine consumer attitudes as part of a Business Studies course, urban land use as part of a Geography course, or gender relations as part of a Psychology or Sociology course.

PLANNING RESEARCH

Before starting your research be sure to make a plan. Begin with a careful analysis of any documents that detail the requirements and objectives of your coursework and, in particular, that clarify how your coursework will be assessed and marked. When planning research it is also important to recognise any financial, time and ethical constraints. For example, if you aim to examine patterns of mobile phone use among students at your school you will not have time to interview every student! You might, however, ask all students in your year group to complete a short questionnaire and then interview, say, three students.

ETHICAL CONSIDERATIONS FOR COURSEWORK

- **Consent** – Gain the full consent of individuals before involving them in research, e.g. before recording a conversation.
- **Confidentiality** – Protect confidentiality by ensuring that individuals are not required to write their names on questionnaires, and that pseudonyms are used when they are quoted in reports.
- **Consequences** – Minimise any potentially negative consequences of your research, e.g. significant disruption to other people's lives.

RESEARCH AIMS

The next step is to clarify the aims of your research. These will determine the methods that you use to collect data, to analyse data and to formulate conclusions from your findings. The panel below gives an example of how to think about research aims.

CLARIFYING RESEARCH AIMS FOR A SOCIOLOGY PROJECT

One way of clarifying research aims is to work towards the creation of a research **title, hypothesis** and a number of **specific aims**.

1. Begin by examining the various units of the specification.

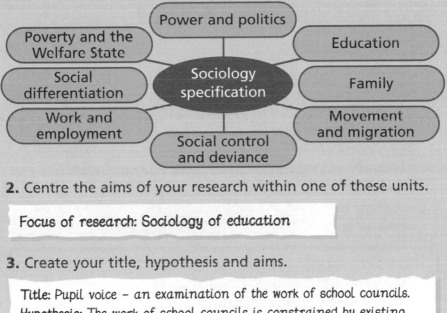

Power and politics

Poverty and the Welfare State

Education

Social differentiation

Sociology specification

Family

Work and employment

Movement and migration

Social control and deviance

2. Centre the aims of your research within one of these units.

Focus of research: Sociology of education

3. Create your title, hypothesis and aims.

Title: Pupil voice - an examination of the work of school councils.
Hypothesis: The work of school councils is constrained by existing teacher–pupil relations at secondary schools.
Aims:

- To identify pupils' perceptions of the work of school councils
- To examine the extent to which school councils are effective democratic structures
- To develop a model of the ideal school council.

DATA COLLECTION: SAMPLING

When attempting to identify the characteristics of a specific population (e.g. visitors to children's playgrounds), you will need to work with a sample from this population. If your aim is to compare the patterns of behaviour at rural playgrounds with those at urban playgrounds then, rather than attempting to collect data at many playgrounds, you could concentrate on observing activities at one village playground and at one town or city playground.

DATA COLLECTION: QUESTIONNAIRES

When designing questionnaires:
- Begin with a brief description of the research aims, with reassurance that all responses will be kept confidential, and with a few non-threatening questions (e.g. gender, age, ethnicity).
- Consider the question type.
  Closed questions have only one or a limited number of possible responses, e.g. 'Circle the number that most closely represents the extent to which you agree with the following statements.'
  Open questions invite extensive and personal responses, e.g. 'Describe the qualities that you think make up a good citizen.'
- Avoid certain types of question:
  Leading questions, e.g. 'Do you agree that eating meat is wrong?'
  Complex questions, e.g. 'Are we living in a post-modern society?'
  Double negatives, e.g. 'Would you disagree that most pupils do not support recycling initiatives?'
  Several questions within a question, e.g. 'What do you think of the fact that in the UK a healthy foetus can be aborted up until the age of 24 weeks and that a disabled foetus can legally be aborted up until the age of 40 weeks?'
- If possible, try to distribute questionnaires in person rather than relying on other people to distribute them.

DATA COLLECTION: INTERVIEWS

Questionnaires are effective when examining broad perspectives within a population. To enable you to gather more in-depth data use:

- **Interviews** – these typically involve one person
- **Focus groups** – these typically involve three to six people.

It is particularly helpful to be able to back up conclusions made from data collected using one research method with data collected using another. This is known as 'triangulation' and enables you to formulate more confident conclusions in the closing sections of your report.

PLANNING AN INTERVIEW

In certain circumstances (e.g. when conducting exploratory research) it is appropriate to conduct completely unstructured interviews. However, for most research you will need to design an **interview schedule** that lists and structures pre-prepared questions to ask interviewees. Always test out interview schedules and questionnaires, perhaps on a few family members or friends, to get some constructive criticism and feedback on the content and design before you use them in your research.

ADVICE ON CONDUCTING AN INTERVIEW

- It is important to maintain eye contact during interviews. Do your best to memorise the questions that you intend to ask and to glance down only occasionally to your interview schedule to keep on track.
- As well as the main questions, you might also like to include a few key words that can act as 'prompts' to encourage you to probe interviewees more deeply when they offer short replies.
- Always record interviews so that you can listen back to responses. If you have time, transcribe recordings so that you have a written record. This is especially helpful during data analysis.

WRITING UP FINDINGS: DATA ANALYSIS

The following analysis methods are most suited to small-scale research.

- **Quantitative data** involves numbers rather than words or observations. It can be analysed using totals, percentages and means.
- **Qualitative data** involves broader statements such as those made during interviews. It can usefully be grouped under headings to create themes. This approach is illustrated below (the interview statements were made during research into levels of parental involvement in secondary schools).

School as a parent-free space

Pupil 1: Apart from it being embarrassing, if parents came in they would just decide everything for us. I wouldn't like them to come in and then watch me doing what I do because I'd feel uncomfortable.

Pupil 2: I'd hate that.

Pupil 3: I mean it might work in pre-school but it wouldn't work here because, you know, pupils would have a go at the parents and then they might have a go at 'Your Dad gave me a detention last week' or something and beat you up over it.

Parent: My two sons. They would hate the thought I'd even cross the school threshold. I'm sure that not all teenagers are like this but a lot like their own space. The thought that parents are invading it I'm not sure would be very successful.

Parent-governor: The children want to grow up and they don't want their parents to have the same type of involvement as they had at primary school. They don't want them there on the doorstep every five minutes. It's their space if you like.

> This heading represents a 'theme' that emerged during the interviews

WRITING UP FINDINGS: REPORT-WRITING
When writing up research projects it is typical to divide reports into at least five sections.

1. In the **introduction** you should introduce the focus of your research, discuss related previous research that you have studied (e.g. in class), and outline your hypothesis and research aims.

2. Within the **methods** section you can then describe the techniques (e.g. questionnaires, observations or interviews) that you used to collect data.

3. In the **results** section you can outline and summarise your findings. During this section it is helpful to include pictorial summaries, for example tables, pie charts, histograms and scatter diagrams.

4. Having discussed the aims, methods and results you should then make tentative **conclusions**. Take care to recognise throughout the constraints under which your research was conducted and to reflect critically on the methods that you used to collect and analyse data.

5. In the **appendices** you can include copies of any research instruments that you used (e.g. questionnaires and interview schedules).

CONSTRUCTIVE FEEDBACK
Remember that your teachers are not allowed to write reports for you, but they can offer advice. It is very important to receive constructive criticism, so make sure that you proactively ask teachers, classmates and family members for ongoing feedback on your progress.

Using ICT when revising

USING THE WWW

The World Wide Web can be used to search and research information and topics.

Use a **browser** to help you to find useful sites. Here are two examples:

- **www.google.co.uk**
- **www.ask.com**

Use Ask Jeeves to find useful websites to help you with your studies

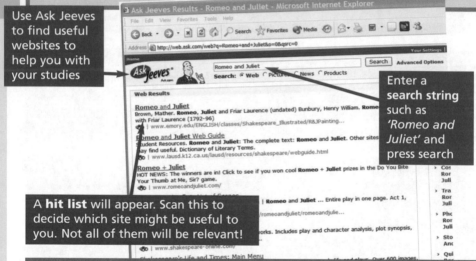

Enter a **search string** such as 'Romeo and Juliet' and press search

A **hit list** will appear. Scan this to decide which site might be useful to you. Not all of them will be relevant!

When you find a site that is useful, make a note of the URL and write a brief description of what was so good about it. Here are some examples:

- **www.howstuffworks.com**
  Lots of information on lots of topics
- **www.bbc.co.uk**
  News and lots of other information
- **the-tech.mit.edu/Shakespeare/romeo_juliet**
  Complete works, includes overview of whole play in one page

Share your useful sites with others on your course – their suggestions may prove very useful to you.

USING APPLICATION SOFTWARE

Standard *Office* applications can help you when revising:

- **Word processing** can be used to create **checklists** from which you can test yourself. You could **highlight** important facts that you need to remember. **Footnotes** provide one way to remind yourself about things you still need to do.
- **Spreadsheets** can be used to set up a **schedule**, with the dates being automatically calculated for you.
- A **database** could be used to record information in a more structured way.
- **Microsoft *Outlook*** includes a **calendar** that you could use to plan your revision. There is also an option to set up **tasks** and **reminders**.

ICT FOR PLANNING

Planning what you will do – and keeping track of your progress – is important. An **action plan** lists everything that you think you need to do, with space for you to note when things need to be done by, and a way of showing what you have – and have not yet – done.

You might create an action plan using a table in *Word* as shown on the next page. If you think of extra things to do, you can insert new rows, so that the 'Do it by' column is in date order. Or, you could use the Table–Sort function to sort the entries into date order. You could print out your action plan. You could then pin it on your notice board, or carry it with you.

The same information could form a task in Microsoft *Outlook*.

REMEMBER

Start each day or week or month by checking each of your action plans – to see what progress you have, and to rethink your plans for the next period of time.

AN ACTION PLAN IN WORD

ACTION PLAN for: February		
Problem area: **GCSE English**	Do it by	DONE!
Arrange to meet Jack for joint revision session	2 Feb	✔
Book tickets to see Romeo and Juliet at Holmwood Theatre	2 Feb	✔
Revision session with Jack	6 Feb	
Go to see theatre production of R&J	7 Feb	
Arrange to meet Mrs Thomas to agree extension of hand-in deadline	9 Feb	
Go to the library and borrow a revision text on *Hard Times*	9 Feb	
Read revision text! Make notes.	13 Feb	
Finish the practice exam essay for R&J	16 Feb	
Check progress on coursework folder	20 Feb	
Finish practice exam question for HT	27 Feb	
Book another session with Jack?	27 Feb	

AN ACTION PLAN IN OUTLOOK

Set up a reminder – and then *Outlook* will automatically remind you to take action

Copy and paste the next action into the Subject line – so it is visible in your task list, as a reminder

Type your list of actions in the body of the task, in date order

2 Feb	Arrange to meet Jack for joint revision session DONE
2 Feb	Book tickets to see Romeo and Juliet at Holmwood Theatre DONE
6 Feb	Revision session with Jack
7 Feb	Go to see theatre production of R&J
9 Feb	Arrange to meet Mrs Thomas to agree extension of hand in deadline
9 Feb	Go to the library and borrow a revision text on Hard Times
13 Feb	Read revision text! Make notes.
16 Feb	Finish the practice exam essay for R&J
20 Feb	Check progress on coursework folder
27 Feb	Finish practice exam question for HT
27 Feb	Book another session with Jack?

When you complete an action, write DONE against it

To insert a new action, type it into the right place within the text so that the date order is maintained

REVISION SCHEDULES

ICT can be used to help in your preparation of revision schedules. Of course, you need to plan your time carefully throughout your revision. But time management needs to continue during the examination weeks, too, so that you have time for resting and recovering from one exam, and then have time to brush up before the next exam.

You could create a table within Microsoft *Word*, or use the calendar feature on software like Microsoft *Outlook* as shown below.

You can look at one day, or a week, or a whole month of appointments

Dates with appointments are shown in bold

Today's date is shown boxed

You set a reminder and make notes for each appointment

Notice the Task Pad – this lists all tasks that you have set up

When planning your revision timetable, first record all the exams that you will be taking

Then, you can think about how to fill the gaps, with revision sessions or with rest periods

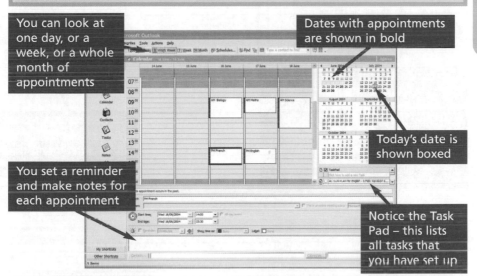

WRITING COURSEWORK REPORTS

If you word-process your coursework, and apply **styles**, your document will automatically be structured.

This means you can look at your work in **outline view** to check that you have included all the sections that you want, and that they are at the right level.

Write your report in sections

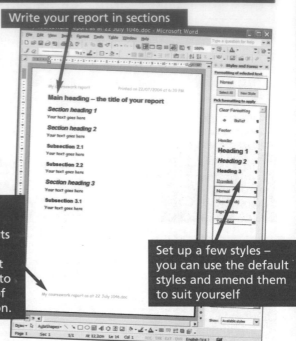

Use the document header and footer to record important information. Then your printouts will show clearly what your document is called, and when it was printed. This will help you to keep track of revised versions of your work and show progression.

Set up a few styles – you can use the default styles and amend them to suit yourself

Using styles also means you can create a **contents list** automatically.

Select View–Outline

Decide what level of heading you want to see

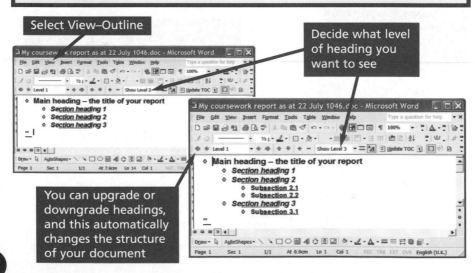

You can upgrade or downgrade headings, and this automatically changes the structure of your document

So, you can then use the Contents list to help you to plan your coursework.

Select Insert–Reference–Index and Tables and then click on the Table of Contents tab

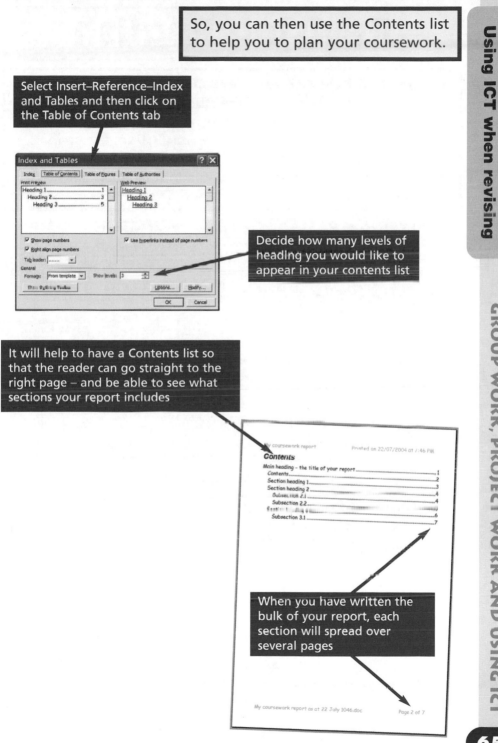

Decide how many levels of heading you would like to appear in your contents list

It will help to have a Contents list so that the reader can go straight to the right page – and be able to see what sections your report includes

When you have written the bulk of your report, each section will spread over several pages

Revising English

ANALYSING DIFFERENT TYPES OF TEXT

GCSE English courses now require students to show evidence that they can analyse a wide variety of texts (e.g. classic literature, modern literature, fiction, non-fiction, newspapers, and adverts). This section focuses on the analysis of advertisements to illustrate how you might develop and memorise checklists for different types of text.

ANALYSING A PASSAGE OF TEXT ON ENGLISH

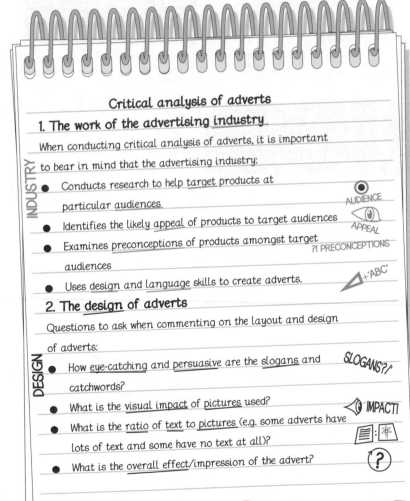

Critical analysis of adverts

1. The work of the advertising industry

When conducting critical analysis of adverts, it is important to bear in mind that the advertising industry:

INDUSTRY
- Conducts research to help target products at particular audiences.   ◉ AUDIENCE
- Identifies the likely appeal of products to target audiences   👁 APPEAL
- Examines preconceptions of products amongst target audiences   ?! PRECONCEPTIONS
- Uses design and language skills to create adverts.   △+'ABC'

2. The design of adverts

Questions to ask when commenting on the layout and design of adverts:

DESIGN
- How eye-catching and persuasive are the slogans and catchwords?   SLOGANS?
- What is the visual impact of pictures used?   ◁ IMPACT!
- What is the ratio of text to pictures (e.g. some adverts have lots of text and some have no text at all)?   📄:🎴
- What is the overall effect/impression of the advert?   (?)

3. The language of adverts

When commenting on language used in adverts, refer to examples of any of the following linguistic devices:

LANGUAGE

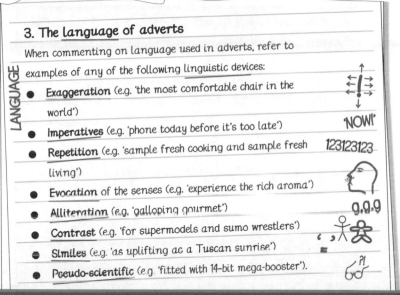

- **Exaggeration** (e.g. 'the most comfortable chair in the world')
- **Imperatives** (e.g. 'phone today before it's too late')
- **Repetition** (e.g. 'sample fresh cooking and sample fresh living')
- **Evocation** of the senses (e.g. 'experience the rich aroma')
- **Alliteration** (e.g. 'galloping gourmet')
- **Contrast** (e.g. 'for supermodels and sumo wrestlers')
- **Similes** (e.g. 'as uplifting as a Tuscan sunrise.')
- **Pseudo-scientific** (e.g. 'fitted with 14-bit mega-booster').

USING SUMMARY SHAPES TO REVISE ENGLISH

You have studied the passage of text offering guidance on conducting a critical analysis of adverts.

You know that your ability to recall these points will offer a helpful framework when answering questions related to adverts in your exams. You therefore decide to create a summary circle to help you to remember the main points.

A SUMMARY CIRCLE ON THE CRITICAL ANALYSIS OF ADVERTS

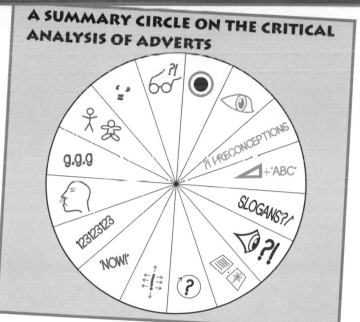

USING MNEMONICS TO REVISE ENGLISH

The passage of text identified eight linguistic devices to which you might refer when commenting on language used in adverts:

- Exaggeration
- Imperatives
- Repetition
- Evocation
- Alliteration
- Contrast
- Similes
- Pseudo-scientific language.

To develop a mnemonic that will help you to remember these eight devices you could run through the thought process shown below.

As these are all language devices, I could begin my mnemonic by imagining that I meet a female cartoon character with huge lips (i.e. used to form language). As soon as I meet this cartoon character she tells me how rich, attractive and clever that she is (exaggeration) and to get out of her way NOW (imperatives). Bizarrely, she soon forgets this order and, once again, tells me how very rich, attractive and clever she is (repetition). She then sprays herself with perfume that smells so strong that it gives me a coughing fit (evocation of the senses) and her only response is to say 'silly, sneezy, soft and squeezy' (alliteration). She introduces me to her thin-lipped husband who is extremely shy (contrast) and apologises that he is always 'as quiet as a mouse' (simile). I ask her husband whether or not he has a job. He says that he is currently busy designing a 48-bit digitally enhanced virtual marmite downloader (pseudo-scientific).

REMEMBER
Mnemonics of this sort are best learnt and
reinforced by acting them out.
- Visualise the story in your mind's eye.
- Speak through it aloud.
- When acting, exaggerate each movement like a
  mime-artist.

Have fun!

USING SUMMARY MAPS TO LEARN ENGLISH
In order to record a more detailed summary of guidance on
the critical analysis of adverts, you could use the key words
that you underlined and the annotations that you wrote in the
margins to create a summary map.

A SUMMARY MAP ON THE CRITICAL
ANALYSIS OF ADVERTS

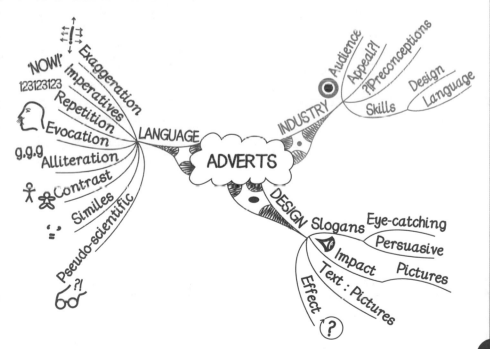

Revising Maths

PREPARING FOR PROBLEM-SOLVING

Maths courses are made up of lots of short topics. When revising Maths, develop a collection of concise summary sheets to which you can refer when solving problems, and especially during last-minute revision in the run-up to your exams. When developing summary sheets of this sort it is very important to use colour and to create headings that remind you of *when* to apply a particular rule or formula.

MEMORISING FORMULAE

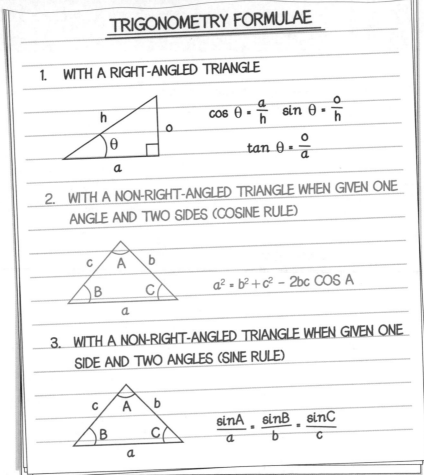

TRIGONOMETRY FORMULAE

1. WITH A RIGHT-ANGLED TRIANGLE

$$\cos \theta = \frac{a}{h} \quad \sin \theta = \frac{o}{h}$$

$$\tan \theta = \frac{o}{a}$$

2. WITH A NON-RIGHT-ANGLED TRIANGLE WHEN GIVEN ONE ANGLE AND TWO SIDES (COSINE RULE)

$$a^2 = b^2 + c^2 - 2bc \cos A$$

3. WITH A NON-RIGHT-ANGLED TRIANGLE WHEN GIVEN ONE SIDE AND TWO ANGLES (SINE RULE)

$$\frac{\sin A}{a} = \frac{\sin B}{b} = \frac{\sin C}{c}$$

PROBLEM-SOLVING SKILLS

To ensure that you are prepared to solve problems under exam conditions, when revising Maths get into the habit of working through the following steps to help develop strong problem-solving skills.

Step 1: Underline key words and figures in the question to clarify information that you are given or asked.

Step 2: Take a minute to think through the question and complete some initial workings.

Step 3: Identify the topic to which the question refers.

Step 4: Write down concepts or formulae that you need in order to answer this question.

Step 5: Answer the question, showing your working.

EXAMPLE 1: TRIGONOMETRY

Step 1: Underline key words and figures

A boat leaves port and sails <u>75 miles</u> due <u>west.</u> It then changes direction and sails <u>65 miles</u> on a bearing of <u>150°.</u> <u>How far</u> from the <u>port</u> is the boat now?

Step 2: Initial thoughts/workings

Step 3: Identify topic

Trigonometry

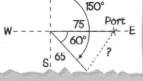

Step 4: Write down concepts and formulae

Trigonometry formulae for non-right angled triangles (cosine rule)

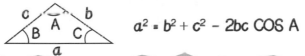

$$a^2 = b^2 + c^2 - 2bc \cos A$$

Step 5: Answer question showing working

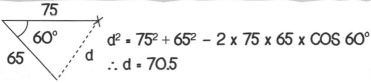

$$d^2 = 75^2 + 65^2 - 2 \times 75 \times 65 \times \cos 60°$$
$$\therefore d = 70.5$$

The boat is 70.5 miles away from the port.

EXAMPLE 2: PROCESSING AND REPRESENTING DATA

Step 1: Underline key words and figures

45 students were asked how long it took them to travel to school. The results (recorded in minutes) are shown below:

Time (min)	0<x≤10	10<x≤20	20<x≤30	30<x≤40	40<x≤50
Frequency	25	5	3	10	2

a) Write down the modal class.

b) Calculate an estimate for the mean time.

Step 2: Initial thoughts/workings

a) Mode happens most.

b) Estimated mean is the sum of fx divided by total frequency.

Step 3: Identify topic

Finding mean, median and mode of grouped data.

Step 4: Write down concepts and formulae

a) Modal class has highest frequency.

b) Estimated mean = $\dfrac{\sum fx}{\sum f}$ where f is frequency and x is mid-value

Step 5: Answer question showing working

a) **0<x≤10** has highest frequency and is therefore the modal class.

b) To find the mean:

Time (min)	Frequency f	Mid-value x	fx
0<x≤10	25	(0 + 10)/2 = 5	25 x 5 = 125
10<x≤20	5	(10 + 20)/2 = 15	5 x 15 = 75
20<x≤30	3	(20 + 30)/2 = 25	3 x 25 = 75
30<x≤40	10	(30 + 40)/2 = 35	10 x 35 = 350
40<x≤50	2	(40 + 50)/2 = 45	2 x 45 = 90
Totals	45	NA	715

Estimated mean = $\dfrac{715}{45}$ = 15.9 minutes

MATHEMATICAL MNEMONICS

There are loads of opportunities available to use mnemonics when revising Maths, and in particular through the use of links/association. Here are a couple of examples.

When required to sketch a quadratic function (e.g. $y = ax^2+bx+c$), you need to know whether its parabola (the graph of the quadratic function) faces <u>upwards</u> or faces <u>downwards</u>. The direction of the parabola is given by a.

1) When a is negative (sad) the parabola is downwards.

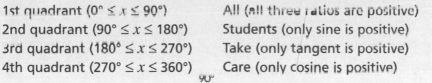 $a<0$

2) When a is positive (happy) the parabola is upwards.

$a>0$

When solving a trigonometric equation (e.g. $3 \sin x = 2$ for $0° \leq x \leq 360°$) your calculator will only give you the solution for the first quadrant ($0° \leq x \leq 90°$). You therefore need to know in which of the other quadrants other solutions might lie. For each quadrant you therefore need to know whether or not the sign of cosine, sine and tangent are positive. The following mnemonic is helpful:

1st quadrant ($0° \leq x \leq 90°$)   All (all three ratios are positive)
2nd quadrant ($90° \leq x \leq 180°$)   Students (only sine is positive)
3rd quadrant ($180° \leq x \leq 270°$)   Take (only tangent is positive)
4th quadrant ($270° \leq x \leq 360°$)   Care (only cosine is positive)

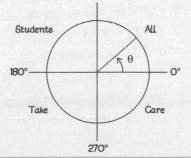

Revising Science

THINKING AND REASONING SCIENTIFICALLY

GCSE Science requires students not only to develop a thorough knowledge and understanding of scientific principles and concepts, but also to show evidence that they can apply this to the process of thinking and reasoning scientifically. This section focuses on a particular topic, ionic bonding, to illustrate how best to revise Science and how to begin to think and reason more scientifically.

ANALYSING A PASSAGE OF TEXT ON SCIENCE

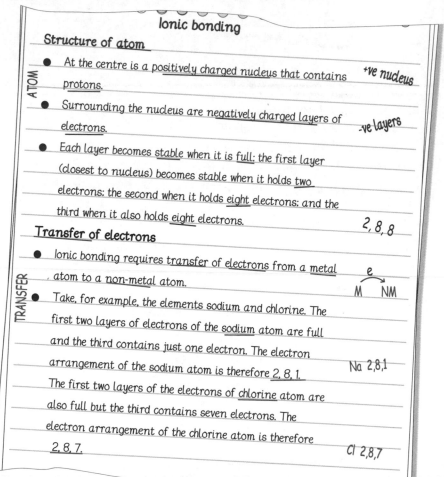

Ionic bonding

Structure of atom

ATOM

- At the centre is a positively charged nucleus that contains protons.   +ve nucleus

- Surrounding the nucleus are negatively charged layers of electrons.   -ve layers

- Each layer becomes stable when it is full: the first layer (closest to nucleus) becomes stable when it holds two electrons: the second when it holds eight electrons: and the third when it also holds eight electrons.   2, 8, 8

Transfer of electrons

TRANSFER

- Ionic bonding requires transfer of electrons from a metal atom to a non-metal atom.
  e
  M → NM

- Take, for example, the elements sodium and chlorine. The first two layers of electrons of the sodium atom are full and the third contains just one electron. The electron arrangement of the sodium atom is therefore 2, 8, 1.   Na 2,8,1

  The first two layers of the electrons of chlorine atom are also full but the third contains seven electrons. The electron arrangement of the chlorine atom is therefore 2, 8, 7.   Cl 2,8,7

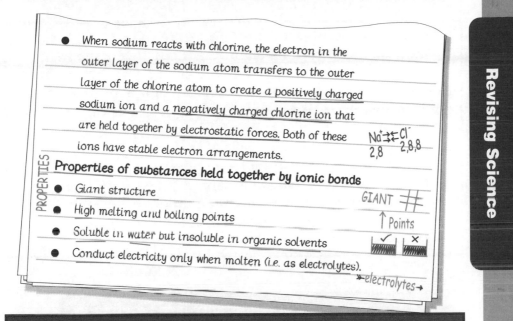

- When sodium reacts with chlorine, the electron in the outer layer of the sodium atom transfers to the outer layer of the chlorine atom to create a positively charged sodium ion and a negatively charged chlorine ion that are held together by electrostatic forces. Both of these ions have stable electron arrangements.

Na⁺ ⋛ Cl⁻
2,8   2,8,8

PROPERTIES

Properties of substances held together by ionic bonds

- Giant structure — GIANT #
- High melting and boiling points — ↑ Points
- Soluble in water but insoluble in organic solvents — ✓ | ✗
- Conduct electricity only when molten (i.e. as electrolytes). ➤electrolytes→

USING SUMMARY SHAPES TO REVISE SCIENCE

The six-point star below is a distinct summary of the passage of text on ionic bonding. All of the information in the sections entitled 'structure of atom' and 'transfer of electrons' is represented by two concise diagrams at the tips of two points of this star. The four 'properties of substances held together by ionic bonds' are represented by key words and symbols at the tips of the remaining four points of this star.

A SUMMARY STAR ON IONIC BONDING

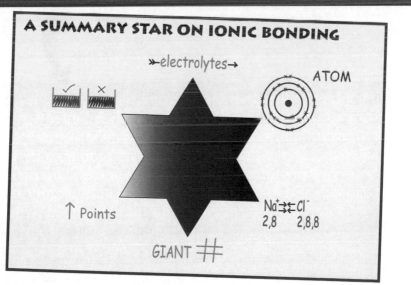

➤electrolytes→

ATOM

↑ Points

Na⁺ ⋛ Cl⁻
2,8   2,8,8

GIANT #

USING MNEMONICS TO REVISE SCIENCE

The principles on which mnemonics are based (e.g. multi-sensory symbols) are useful when revising Science. For example, the passage of text listed four properties typical of substances held together by ionic bonds:

1. Giant structure
2. High melting and boiling points
3. Soluble in water but insoluble in organic solvents
4. Conduct electricity when molten.

You might therefore run through the thought process below to create a mnemonic that will help you to remember these properties.

1. An example of a substance held together by ionic bonding is salt. I could therefore begin my mnemonic with a pot of table salt.

2. The four properties relate to:
1) structure, 2) heat, 3) solubility, 4) conductivity.

3. To help remember these four properties, I could therefore imagine a pot of salt sitting on my kitchen table that:
1) Transforms into a toy skyscraper (giant structure)
2) Remains completely unaffected by attempts to destroy it with a flamethrower (high melting and boiling points)
3) Disappears when thrown into a bucket of water (soluble in water) but returns when this bucket is filled with a strong smelling liquid (insoluble in organic solvents)
4) Gives me an electric shock when I melt it in a saucepan (conducts electricity when molten).

4. In order to keep a written record of this mnemonic, I could draw a rough sketch to keep in my Science file.

5. I could also review and reinforce this mnemonic by replacing the pot of salt with another salty object (e.g. a bag of crisps).

USING SUMMARY MAPS TO REVISE SCIENCE

To record a more detailed summary of the passage on ionic bonding, use the key words that you underlined and the annotations that you wrote in the margins to help create a summary map.

A SUMMARY MAP ON IONIC BONDING

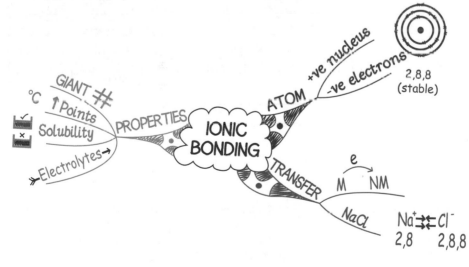

Revising Modern Foreign Languages

LEARNING VOCABULARY

GCSE modern foreign language courses are typically divided into themes such as:

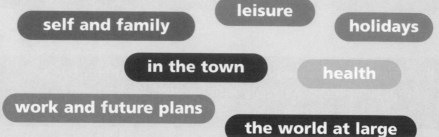

self and family

leisure

holidays

in the town

health

work and future plans

the world at large

In order to answer questions related to these themes, students need to be familiar with certain vocabulary.

In the example opposite, a summary wheel has been used to divide a list of 30 French words on 'self and family' into six manageable sub-sets. Different colours have been used to differentiate words according to their gender (i.e. blue for male and red for female).

When revising vocabulary in this way, create two summary shapes (i.e. one in the target language and one in English) for each topic. You can then use these as prompts to help test your knowledge. It is important not only that you can translate from the target language into English (for listening and reading exams) but also that you can translate from English into the target language (for spoken and written exams).

A SUMMARY WHEEL OF 'SELF AND FAMILY' WORDS

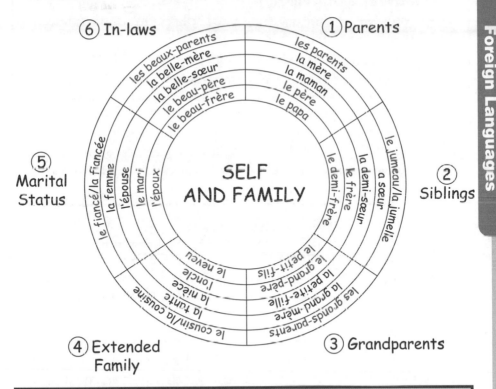

⑥ In-laws
les beaux-parents
la belle-mère
la belle-sœur
le beau-père
le beau-frère

① Parents
les parents
la mère
la maman
le père
le papa

⑤ Marital Status
le fiancé/la fiancée
la femme
l'épouse
le mari
l'époux

SELF AND FAMILY

② Siblings
le jumeau/la jumelle
la sœur
la demi-sœur
le frère
le demi-frère

④ Extended Family
le cousin/la cousine
la tante
la nièce
l'oncle
le neveu

③ Grandparents
les grands-parents
le grand-père
la grand-mère
la petite-fille
le petit-fils

MORE PRACTICE

This example only uses nouns. Create similar but separate summary wheels using adjectives, adverbs and verbs. For practice, have a go at grouping the following nine verbs into three groups of related words in order to create a simple three-part summary wheel of verbs related to the topic 'self and family':

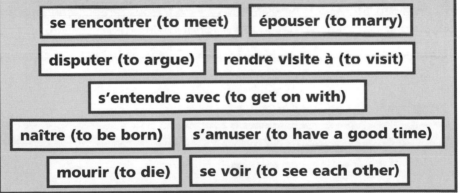

se rencontrer (to meet)	épouser (to marry)
disputer (to argue)	rendre visite à (to visit)
s'entendre avec (to get on with)	
naître (to be born)	s'amuser (to have a good time)
mourir (to die)	se voir (to see each other)

USING DIFFERENT TENSES

When completing their written and spoken language exams, students are more likely to be awarded high grades if they (accurately) use different tenses. Get into the habit of translating sentences into past, present and future tenses. One approach is to use a computer to create, say, a three-columned table (you could use four or five columns if you feel confident enough to use more tenses). You can use the left-hand column for past tenses, move to the centre column for present tenses and then move to the right-hand column for future tenses.

Past	Present	Future
She had pink hair. Elle avait les cheveux roses.	She has pink hair. Elle a les cheveux roses.	She will have pink hair. Elle aura les cheveux roses.
They were really excited. Ils étaient vraiment excités.	They are really excited. Ils sont vraiment excités.	They will be really excited. Ils seront vraiment excités.
I went surfing in Cornwall. J'ai fait du surf aux Cornouailles.	I am going surfing in Cornwall. Je fais du surf aux Cornouailles.	I will go surfing in Cornwall. Je ferai du surf aux Cornouailles.
We made a lot of noise. Nous avons fait beaucoup de bruit.	We make a lot of noise. Nous faisons beaucoup de bruit.	We will make a lot of noise. Nous ferons beaucoup de bruit.
He played for England. Il a joué pour l'Angleterre.	He plays for England. Il joue pour l'Angleterre.	He will play for England. Il jouera pour l'Angleterre.

USING MORE COMPLEX SENTENCES

Students tend to achieve higher marks if they (accurately) use more complex sentences in their written and spoken exams. Practise developing sentences that use several tenses and that use vocabulary from different topic areas (e.g. 'self and family' as well as 'holidays' or 'leisure').

One way of doing this is to write out all of the nouns that you need to know and all of the verbs that you need to know. Cut out the words and put the nouns in one box and the verbs in another box. You can then play 'bingo' by picking out, say, three nouns and two verbs before trying to construct sentences using these words. Remember also to try to use more than one tense. Here is an example.

S'entendre bien avec (*to get on well with*)

La grand-mère (*grandmother*)   **Le frère (*brother*)**

L'argent (*money*)   **Faire du ski (*to go skiing*)**

Ma grand-mère m'a donné de l'argent pour mon anniversaire, alors j'ai décidé de faire du ski avec mon frère car je m'entends vraiment bien avec lui.
(My grandmother gave me some money for my birthday so I decided to go skiing with my brother because I get on really well with him.)

MORE PRACTICE

When completing the written exam, students are often required to write short passages of formal correspondence (e.g. a cover letter for a job application) and informal correspondence (e.g. a postcard or letter to a pen-friend). Pick out more words (e.g. 15 nouns and 10 verbs) and use these to help practise constructing short passages of correspondence of this sort.

Revising History

UNDERSTANDING HISTORICAL CIRCUMSTANCES

GCSE History courses typically require students to develop and strengthen their memory and understanding of poignant and prolonged circumstances experienced in different parts of the world over the last century (e.g. the First World War, the Second World War, the Cold War and the collapse of communism). This section illustrates how you might use summary shapes, summary maps and mnemonics to revise History topics.

ANALYSING A PASSAGE OF TEXT ON HISTORY

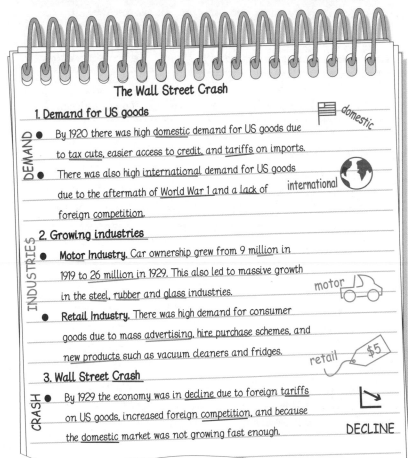

The Wall Street Crash

1. Demand for US goods

DEMAND

- By 1920 there was high domestic demand for US goods due to tax cuts, easier access to credit, and tariffs on imports.   domestic
- There was also high international demand for US goods due to the aftermath of World War 1 and a lack of foreign competition.   international

2. Growing industries

INDUSTRIES

- Motor Industry. Car ownership grew from 9 million in 1919 to 26 million in 1929. This also led to massive growth in the steel, rubber and glass industries.   motor
- Retail Industry. There was high demand for consumer goods due to mass advertising, hire purchase schemes, and new products such as vacuum cleaners and fridges.   retail $5

3. Wall Street Crash

CRASH

- By 1929 the economy was in decline due to foreign tariffs on US goods, increased foreign competition, and because the domestic market was not growing fast enough.   DECLINE

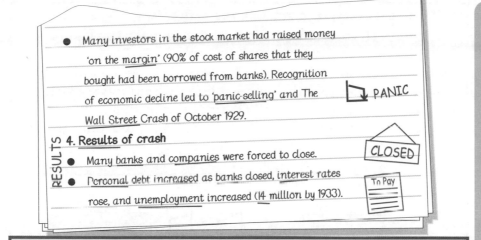

- Many investors in the stock market had raised money 'on the margin' (90% of cost of shares that they bought had been borrowed from banks). Recognition of economic decline led to 'panic-selling' and The Wall Street Crash of October 1929.

↓ PANIC

RESULTS

4. Results of crash

- Many banks and companies were forced to close.

△ CLOSED

- Personal debt increased as banks closed, interest rates rose, and unemployment increased (14 million by 1933).

To Pay

USING SUMMARY SHAPES TO REVISE HISTORY

The eight-part summary circle below summarises key information from the passage of text on The Wall Street Crash.

- Different colours are used to distinguish between each of the four main sections.
- Symbols from the margins are used to represent particular facts.
- Key words are used to reinforce the focus of each of the eight bullet-points.

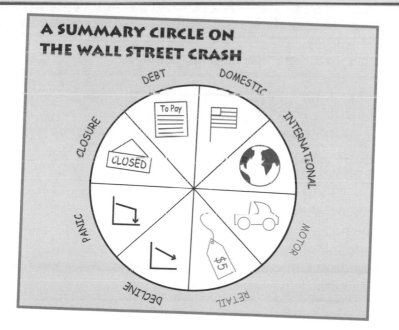

A SUMMARY CIRCLE ON THE WALL STREET CRASH

USING MNEMONICS TO REVISE HISTORY

One approach to revising History is to view each topic as a sequence of events and circumstances that need to be remembered and understood. Timelines and memory journeys are therefore particularly helpful when revising this subject. The passage of text on The Wall Street Crash could, for example, be divided up into eight parts (using the eight bullet-points) to create an eight-part timeline:

To help you remember this timeline and topic, the eight symbols used above could each be placed at eight landmarks on an imaginary memory journey. Let's say, for example, that every time you travel from your home to your school you pass the following eight landmarks: 1) a war memorial; 2) a playground; 3) a tall tree; 4) a pond; 5) a post-office; 6) a train station; 7) a night-club; and 8) the gates of your school. You could then place each of the eight symbols appearing in the timeline at each landmark to imagine an extraordinary memory journey:

1. A giant American flag blowing in the wind above the war memorial.
2. A huge globe spinning in the middle of the playground.
3. Vintage cars stacked-up as tall as the tree.
4. Thousands of price labels floating in the pond.
5. An arrow pointing downwards on the front of the post-office.
6. People running around in panic at the train station.
7. The word 'closed' written in red on the door of the night-club.
8. A huge bill pinned to the front of the school gates.

Create your own memory journeys and ask a friend to test you to see how much you can remember!

USING SUMMARY MAPS TO REVISE HISTORY

In order to record a more detailed summary of the passage of text on The Wall Street Crash, you could use the key words that you underlined and the annotations that you wrote in the margins of this text to create a summary map.

A SUMMARY MAP ON THE WALL STREET CRASH

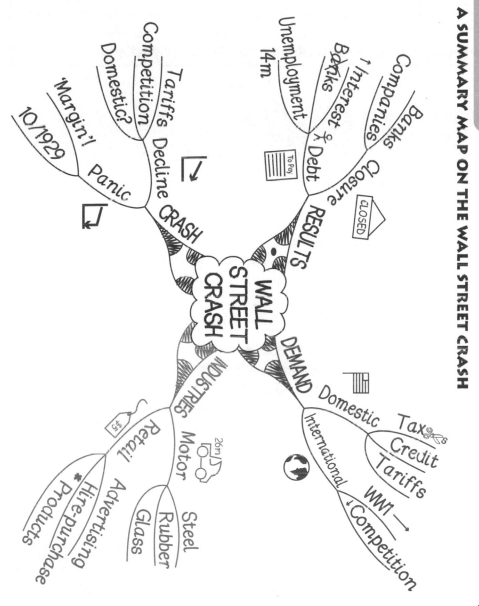

Revising Geography

UNDERSTANDING GEOGRAPHICAL PROCESSES

GCSE Geography courses require students to develop a comprehensive memory, knowledge and understanding of geographical processes. This section focuses on how you might revise a topical geographical process, global warming, to illustrate how best to revise your Geography syllabus.

ANALYSING A PASSAGE OF TEXT ON GEOGRAPHY

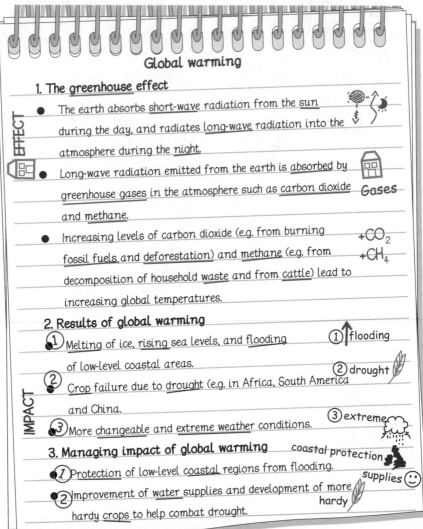

Global warming

EFFECT

1. The greenhouse effect
- The earth absorbs short-wave radiation from the sun during the day, and radiates long-wave radiation into the atmosphere during the night.
- Long-wave radiation emitted from the earth is absorbed by greenhouse gases in the atmosphere such as carbon dioxide and methane.   Gases
- Increasing levels of carbon dioxide (e.g. from burning fossil fuels and deforestation) and methane (e.g. from decomposition of household waste and from cattle) lead to increasing global temperatures. $+CO_2$ $+CH_4$

IMPACT

2. Results of global warming
① Melting of ice, rising sea levels, and flooding of low-level coastal areas.   ① flooding
② Crop failure due to drought (e.g. in Africa, South America and China.   ② drought
③ More changeable and extreme weather conditions.   ③ extreme

3. Managing impact of global warming   coastal protection
① Protection of low-level coastal regions from flooding.
② Improvement of water supplies and development of more hardy crops to help combat drought.   supplies ☺ hardy

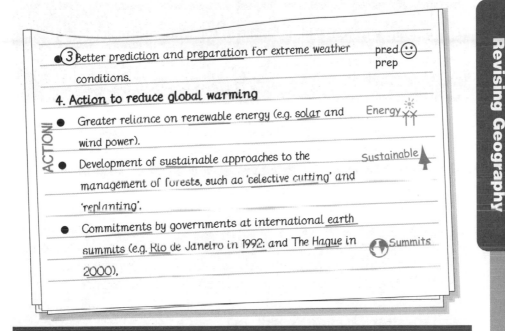

- ③ Better prediction and preparation for extreme weather conditions.   pred 😊 prep

4. Action to reduce global warming

ACTION!

- Greater reliance on renewable energy (e.g. solar and wind power).   Energy ☀
- Development of sustainable approaches to the management of forests, such as 'selective cutting' and 'replanting'.   Sustainable 🌲
- Commitments by governments at international earth summits (e.g. Rio de Janeiro in 1992; and The Hague in 2000).   🌍 Summits

USING SUMMARY SHAPES TO REVISE GEOGRAPHY

Although the passage on global warming includes 12 bullet-points, closer inspection suggests that the section on the greenhouse effect can be represented as a single diagram, and that the sections on the results of global warming and managing the impact of global warming refer to the same issues (i.e. rising sea levels, drought and extreme weather). A triangle can therefore be used to help summarise this text.

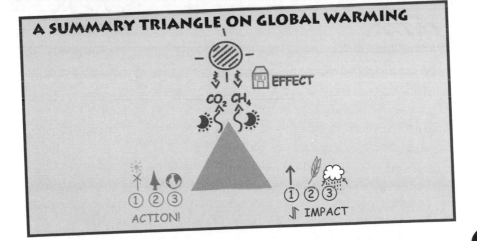

A SUMMARY TRIANGLE ON GLOBAL WARMING

USING MNEMONICS TO REVISE GEOGRAPHY

Mnemonics are particularly helpful when revising geographical processes. You could run through the following thoughts to develop a mnemonic that sums up the greenhouse effect described in the text.

- There were four variables mentioned: short-waves, long-waves, carbon dioxide and methane.
- I could represent short-waves as short yellow strands of string because they come from the sun, long-waves as long brown strands because they come from the earth, carbon dioxide as a green petrol-smelling cloud because it comes from deforestation and burning fossil fuels, and methane as a foul-smelling black and white cloud because it comes from the decomposition of household waste and from cattle.
- I can draw a sketch to help make a record of this mnemonic:

Short-waves radiated by sun and absorbed by earth during day

Long-waves radiated by earth and absorbed by greenhouse gases at night

- To remember that the short-waves travel during the day, and long-waves at night, I could imagine that when day breaks thousands of short yellow strands of string fall to earth and that when night falls thousands of long brown strands of string rise up to the sky.
- I could also imagine millions of people sweating beneath bulging clouds to represent the rise in global temperature resulting from increased absorption of long-wave radiation by increased levels of carbon dioxide and methane.

USING SUMMARY MAPS TO REVISE GEOGRAPHY

In order to create a more detailed and comprehensive summary of the passage of text on global warming, you could use the key words that you underlined and the annotations that you made in the margins to create a summary map.

A SUMMARY MAP ON GLOBAL WARMING

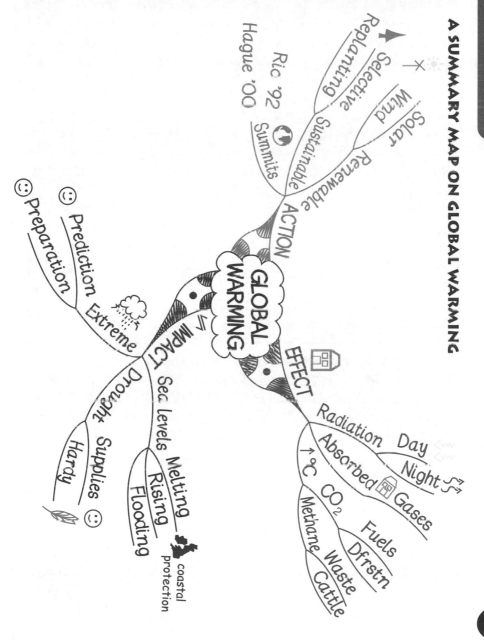

Exam technique

FINAL PREPARATIONS

As soon as possible: Visit the room in which you will take your exams to familiarise yourself with this environment. Remember that you are highly unlikely to gain free access to this space once the examination period begins. It is especially helpful to visit at a quiet time of day so that you can imagine yourself entering and sitting in this room feeling relaxed, alert, focused and confident. This will help you to dissolve fears of what can otherwise appear to be an unknown and very threatening place. Repeat the visit a couple of weeks before exams start.

The weeks before: Use the experience above as a basis for positive visualisation exercises. Focus on enjoying a relaxed and successful experience of each exam.

The week before: Take regular exercise and get to bed early on nights before exams. Make every effort to maintain good physical and mental health during the final stages of your revision and preparation for GCSEs.

The day before: There is nothing wrong with flicking through your notes (e.g. the summary sheets that you have made when revising) and testing yourself the night and morning before exams.

The day before: Avoid activities that create unnecessary tension and set aside plenty of time to maintain and restore a sense of relaxed focus. It is especially helpful to get plenty of fresh air, to breathe deeply and to stretch.

The hour before: Avoid conversations that might distract you away from the task at hand. Focus instead on imagining the likely format and content of the exam paper and the approach that you will adopt when completing this exam.

LOOKING THROUGH PAST EXAM PAPERS

It is essential that you familiarise yourself with the format of each exam paper. As far in advance of your exams as possible, ask your teachers to confirm the exact names of exam boards and papers that you are taking, and if possible to provide you with copies of several past papers or to let you know how to obtain these from exam boards.

Before taking a closer look at past papers, find out whether the format is due to change in any way this year. Ask your teachers or the exam board. Bearing their reply in mind, then complete a close analysis of the format of past papers. In particular, pay close attention to:

- Any initial instructions or guidance
- The names of different sections
- The number of different sections
- Which sections are optional and which are compulsory
- The types of questions asked (e.g. multiple choice, structured short answer, long answer, essays)
- Any topics or questions that appear to crop up each year
- The marking scheme (e.g. the total number of marks allocated to individual questions and to each section)
- The total amount of time available to answer each section
- Commonly used key words (e.g. describe, explain, compare).

If you are unclear in any way about the requirements of any of the papers then do not hesitate to ask your teachers or exam boards to clarify your queries. They will be able to offer you more comprehensive and detailed advice than the exam invigilators.

ALLOCATING LIMITED TIME

Perhaps the most challenging aspect of answering questions under exam conditions is the need to work within strict time constraints. When you practise answering questions from past papers, limit yourself to the total amount of time made available in exams. Practise quickly identifying how much time is available to answer sections or questions. Here is an example for a GCSE History paper:

GCSE History: Paper 1

Time available: 2 hours

Answer questions in TWO of the following choice of six sections. For each section answer part (a) and EITHER part (b) OR part (c).

Section 1: History of industry	**Total marks: 55**
Section 2: History of agriculture	**Total marks: 55**
Section 3: History of transport and leisure	**Total marks: 55**
Section 4: History of health	**Total marks: 55**
Section 5: History of education	**Total marks: 55**
Section 6: History of politics	**Total marks: 55**

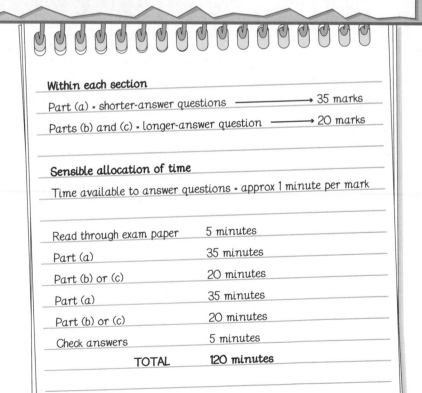

Within each section

Part (a) - shorter-answer questions ⟶ 35 marks

Parts (b) and (c) - longer-answer question ⟶ 20 marks

Sensible allocation of time

Time available to answer questions - approx 1 minute per mark

Read through exam paper	5 minutes
Part (a)	35 minutes
Part (b) or (c)	20 minutes
Part (a)	35 minutes
Part (b) or (c)	20 minutes
Check answers	5 minutes
TOTAL	**120 minutes**

ANSWERING THE QUESTION

When allocating the time available within an exam, always set aside 5–10 minutes for reading through the questions and for planning. Take very great care to read and analyse questions carefully before formulating answers. Misreading even a single word can have serious consequences. For example:

> Explain how agricultural practices have changed over the past 20 years in developed countries.

Here, you are unlikely to receive any marks for explaining how agricultural practices have changed over the last 20 years in <u>developing</u> countries.

It is especially tempting to answer the questions that you would have really liked to have been asked rather than questions that you have actually been asked! Contrary to misconceptions, examiners are required to adhere to strict marking criteria and cannot therefore award marks even to the most extensive and impressive of irrelevant answers. Underline and pay especially close attention to key command words. Identify the type of question you are being asked:

- Descriptive questions tend to require the observation or recall of facts, e.g. 'Describe what Source A says about levels of unemployment in the USA in the 1930s'.
- Evaluative questions tend to require the explanation of causes and processes, e.g. 'Explain the causes and consequences of the Wall Street Crash'.

Command words

describe   explain   compare   choose   list
what   when   where   how   why

Always mentally rehearse answers to questions before writing anything. This will help to keep later corrections and amendments to a minimum. During this process, try to ensure that answers are as relevant, precise and thorough as possible.

LONGER-ANSWER QUESTIONS

When responding to longer-answer questions, you will need to make more comprehensive plans. It can prove especially helpful to sketch out versions of summary sheets that you have been revising as a basis to such plans. When preparing, for example, to answer the question 'Explain the causes and consequences of the Wall Street Crash' you might spend a couple of minutes making a rough sketch of the summary map on this topic outlined in the 'Revising History' section on page 85:

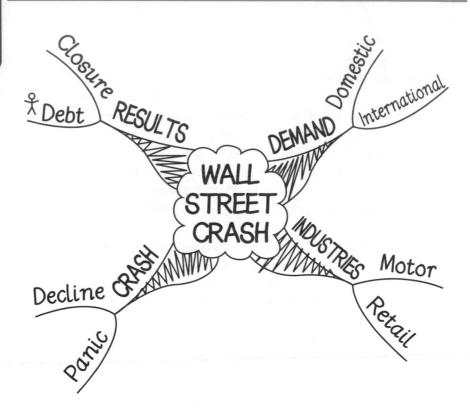

Some other hints on responding to longer-answer questions:
- Keep to the question, to your plan and to time.
- Write at least one main point per paragraph.
- Use examples to illustrate your statements.
- Define important words.
- Focus on quality rather than quantity.

COMPLETING FINAL CHECKS

When allocating the time available within an exam, always set aside 5–10 minutes at the end to complete final checks. During this time:

- Make sure you have answered all of the questions. Even if you are not sure, you will not be penalised for having a go. It is especially important to answer all multiple choice questions as you will typically have a 15%–25% chance of estimating or guessing the correct answer.
- Ensure that you have answered the actual questions that were asked and that your answers are as relevant, precise and thorough as possible.
- When answering Maths and Science questions, make sure that you have shown all of your working.
- Check your grammar, spelling and punctuation. Examiners can mark students up and down according to the accuracy and fluency of their writing style.
- If you run out of time when answering certain questions then try to jot down relevant key words and half sentences. Examiners may be able to give you a few additional marks for work of this sort.
- If you finish early don't sit around twiddling your thumbs! Use this time to check through your paper carefully to see whether or not there are areas where you could make corrections or improvements.

AFTER THE EXAM

At the end of each exam, feel free to debrief on your experiences with friends. However, don't allow this to degenerate into an unhealthy preoccupation with how you may or may not have performed. After an hour or so, treat this chapter of the exam process as closed and take some rest or begin to focus positively towards your next exam.

Good luck!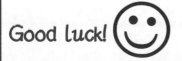

Every effort has been made to contact the holders of copyright material, but if any have been inadvertently overlooked the publishers will be pleased to make the necessary arrangements at the first opportunity.

Published by Letts Educational
The Chiswick Centre
414 Chiswick High Road
London W4 5TF
tel: 020 89963333
fax: 020 87428390
e-mail: mail@lettsed.co.uk
website: www.letts-education.com

Letts Educational Limited is a division of Granada Learning Limited, part of Granada Plc.

Text © James Lee 2005

Design and illustration © Letts Educational Ltd. 2005.

First published 2005

ISBN 184315 4730

British Library Cataloguing in Publication Data

A catalogue record for this book is available from the British Library.

Acknowledgements

Ask Jeeves, Ask.com and the "ask" button are registered trademarks of Ask Jeeves, Inc.

Microsoft Internet Explorer®, Microsoft Office®, Microsoft Outlook Express®, Microsoft Word® are registered trademarks of Microsoft Corporation. Screen shots reprinted by permission from Microsoft Corporation.

Cover design by Big Top.

Commissioned by Cassandra Birmingham.

Project management for Letts by Julia Swales.

Edited by Vicky Butt.

Design and project management by Ken Vail Graphic Design, Cambridge

Printed and bound in Italy.